Duggie Gree...
A Rugby League Sa...

Duggie Greenall proudly wears his first test cap in 1951.

Denis Whittle

London League Publications Ltd

Duggie Greenall
A Rugby League Saint

Front cover photo: Duggie Greenall in action at Knowsley Road in 1952. Back cover photo: Duggie Greenall proudly parades the League Championship trophy following Saints 24-14 win over Halifax at Maine Road, Manchester, in 1953.

A CIP catalogue record for this book is available from the British Library.

First published in Great Britain in September 2006 by:
London League Publications Ltd, P.O. Box 10441, London E14 8WR

ISBN:	(10) 1-903659-27-2
	(13) 9781-903659-27-4
Cover design by:	Stephen McCarthy Graphic Design
	46, Clarence Road, London N15 5BB
Layout:	Peter Lush
Printed & bound by:	Biddles Ltd
	King's Lynn, Norfolk, Great Britain

This book is dedicated to my late wife Margaret and her father Sidney Crank - both true Saints fans and good friends of Duggie.

Foreword

Many youngsters in the immediate post-Second World War period looked to American comics for their heroes. Batman, Superman, the Lone Ranger and even Wonder Woman provided all the thrills and action needed for an outlay of just three pence.

But for most of us living in the shadow of Knowsley Road there was only one hero who could be relied upon to topple the 'Baddie' and snatch triumph from despair. And that was Saints' inspirational centre Duggie Greenall, whose daring deeds could be seen live every Saturday afternoon from the Boys' Pen at the clubhouse end, and for the same cost of three pence

A childhood idol, loved and revered for the ferocity of his tackling and courage in taking on any adversary whatever his size, Saints' test centre soon became a friend and a supporter as I too, many years later, followed him into a St Helens jersey.

A stalwart of the club's Past Players' and British Lions' Associations, Duggie has never lost his enthusiasm for the game of rugby league, and is still as knowledgeable and blessed with the same sense of humour as when he dominated the midfield with his uncanny football skills. Though never blessed with size, opponents feared the venom of his tackles, while wing partners such as Stan McCormick, Steve Llewellyn and the legendary Tom van Vollenhoven were grateful for the full repertoire of his talents in the centre.

Indeed his timing of a pass and instinct when and when not to release his winger was incredible, and more often than not resulted in a try and roars of appreciation and adulation from his fans standing on the popular side at Knowsley Road.

Above all Duggie Greenall was a 'character' who, although he approached his rugby league with deadly seriousness, could always be found displaying his innate sense of fun both on and off the pitch. I am sure that any reader, on learning of Duggie's antics, will realise why a 10-year-old rugby-mad kid like me could supplant Batman (or Robin!) with the unforgettable Duggie Greenall in my preferences for heroes.

Ray French

Ray French was a distinguished player at both rugby codes, and is now one of rugby league's leading journalists and the BBC's rugby league television commentator.

Introduction

'Why me?' was my response when asked to take up the pen on behalf of Douglas Greenall, who is now an hale-and-hearty 79, and still a regular in local supermarkets, if not at Knowsley Road.

I was quickly reminded that I was one of the few surviving scribes of sufficient vintage to remember his Knowsley Road career which spanned the seasons 1946-59.

And now I know how Edmund Hillary and Sherpa Tensing Norgay felt before conquering Everest in the Coronation year of 1953, a period incidentally when Duggie enjoyed one of his greatest triumphs in leading Saints to Championship glory.

Because I realised that I faced a similarly daunting challenge in attempting to relive the life and times of a legendary hard-as nails centre, character extraordinaire, and a player whose name is carved indelibly in Saints' folklore who hung up his boots almost half-a-century ago

Another mountain to climb then, this time for me, in striving to tell the compelling tale of a man who had far more strings to his bow than simply rugby league, and whose physical attributes were described as 11 stones wringing wet and 5 feet 9 inches in stockinged feet - statistics, it would appear, hardly conducive to the hurly-burly of the Greatest Game.

Denis Whittle

About the author

Denis Whittle cut his oval-ball teeth on 'the Bruk' (waste land) near Beechams in St Helens with former Saints' players Josh Gaskell, Roy Robinson and Walter Delves. He attended Lowe House School and has been a Saints' supporter since World War Two, when he carried the team changes board around Knowsley Road. Jim Stott was his boyhood hero and he rates Alex Murphy the greatest player he has seen. Denis met his late wife Margaret on the half-way line at Knowsley Road, and he would like his ashes scattered there, but not just yet. Now a senior citizen, he spent 30 years with the *St Helens Reporter* before joining the *St Helens Star* in 1989. He introduced present chairman Eamonn McManus to the Saints' board and was a contributor to the club programme for many years. He has been on television and radio talking about rugby league and was involved in launching the *Rugby Leaguer* in 1949 as a boy of 16.

Thank you: To Duggie's fellow Saints Ray French, Alex Murphy, Vince Karalius, Austin Rhodes and Glyn Moses; Saints' historian Alex Service and the Saints Heritage Society; Paul Whittle and Norman Clitheroe for enhancing my computer knowledge; and last but certainly not least to the inimitable Duggie for his hilarious co-operation. To Stephen McCarthy for designing the cover, Michael O'Hare for sub-editing, Peter Lush for the layout and Dave Farrar and Peter Lush of London League Publications Ltd for publishing the book.

Contents

Three-point landing!
Duggie Greenall touches down versus Wakefield Trinity
at Knowsley Road in 1951.

1. A rugby league nursery

It was 1927. The country was recovering from the effects of the General Strike, St Helens' Wembley debut lay three years ahead and the immortal Saints winger Alf Ellaby had played his first match at Knowsley Road. And there was similarly eager expectation at the cosy town-centre Churn Inn on Tontine Street on Tuesday 7 June of that year as a bouncing baby boy who was to earn rugby league folk-hero status made his first appearance. Weighing in at a healthy seven pounds two ounces, Douglas Greenall was the first born of licensee Edward and his wife Anne Selina, with his only sibling Teddy arriving some 10 years later. With no midwife available Duggie was delivered by Doctor Archibald Ferrie, who was later appointed surgeon to St Helens Police Force.

Long since demolished to make way for a ring road, Tontine Street was once within the local stockbroker belt, and stood next to St Helens open market in those distant days. It was a closely knit community of teeming terraced houses interspersed by the occasional corner shop plus The Churn, which was a popular watering hole for oval ball devotees.

Duggie was born into rugby league. He was a cousin of Warrington winger Albert Johnson and Saints' flyer Albert 'Sonny' Doyle. Duggie's uncle Dickie Burkhill, a local ice-cream vendor, turned out for Rochdale Hornets as a scrum-half. Duggie is also a descendant of Saints' legend Alf Ellaby.

So it was within this neighbourly working-class backwater that Duggie spent his early boyhood years, with the Greenall family's one concession to elitist education being that their son attended a private school in Arthur Street for a year. "Grandma paid the fees." confided Duggie.

Mum and dad called time on the licensed trade in 1933 and moved to the comparative grandeur of Dunriding Lane next to Saints' ground, where enterprising Mrs Greenall spotted a commercial opportunity by charging fans tuppence to park their bikes in her backyard.

By now Duggie, aged six, was a pupil at St Luke's school, Knowsley Road and, as well as digesting the 'three 'R's, quickly made his mark on the football and cricket fields in captaining both the school and town teams (there was no provision for rugby league at this level).

Gregarious Duggie was also a dedicated member of St Luke's Church Lads Brigade, and was a familiar figure when beating the big drum as the band played the rousing *Olde Edinburgh* march on parish walking days and other festivals – and he still has the pictures to prove it.

In 1938 Duggie was 11 years old and went to Rivington Road School, a rugby league nursery where he soon made friends with the likes of Joe Ball, Bill Finnan, Wilf Roach, George Parr, Ernie Mills and Eddie Cheetham each of whom graduated to play rugby league at St Helens under the guidance of school sports master Harry Cook.

While at Rivington Road Duggie played cricket and football as well as rugby league. He captained the team that won the Waring Cup and was also in the victorious Ellison Cup side skippered by Joe Ball. Parr Central were defeated by a record 45-0, with stand-off Greenall forging a famous half-back link with Ball.

They both appeared in the St Helens town side that won the Lancashire Cup and also earned county selection, such was their uncanny understanding around the base of the scrum in creating openings for speedy threequarters like Mills and Cheetham.

However, the storm clouds of war were hovering and our patriotic 12-year-old enlisted first as a messenger boy for the ARP (Auxiliary Reserve Police) complete with tin hat, and the Air Training Corps, where the commander of 1539 squadron was Harry Cook. The ATC annual sports were an eagerly awaited event with the athletic Duggie regularly among the honours. He particularly remembers winning the gruelling one-mile race. "I never trained for a mini-marathon," he joked, "and was absolutely knackered after running from Rivvy Road to the Carmelite and back."

With desk, inkwell and blackboard now consigned to memory Duggie started work as an apprentice fitter at the Triplex factory, Eccleston, where he was employed on the production of high-explosive shells. "It was a bit dodgy with Jerry bombers lurking overhead en-route to and from Liverpool," added the good-humoured Duggie.

Like father like son! Duggie's dad Ted is caught by the camera on the extreme left of the back row in this memory-jerking shot of amateurs Gerard's Bridge Rovers in 1922.

Rumour also has it that, following a technical miscalculation, Duggie was asked by his boss: "How many thous are there to the inch?" To which our subject replied: "There must be bloody millions."

Duggie was 18 years old in 1945 when the war ended and was liable for military service. He immediately volunteered for a 12-year engagement in the Royal Navy. But a life on the ocean wave was not to be following a Grade 5 medical rating that detected fallen arches on both feet – and he then proceeded to leave defences flat-footed for the following 13 seasons.

When the ATC disbanded Duggie merely played a game of rugby league where he could find one. He made one appearance for St Teresa's, Newtown, on the wing but was not considered good enough. However, such was his love of rugby league that his thirst for a game was unquenchable.

Fortunately he was contacted by Harry Cook, now a director at Saints and later legendary chairman for a record 24 years from 1950 onwards. He suggested that Duggie try his luck at Knowsley Road and the rest, as they say, is history.

The time-honoured old ground - Saints' spiritual home since 1890 - had seen little or no improvement due to wartime austerity, with the stadium crying out for a lick of paint and a general sprucing up.

Rickety wooden stands flanked the touchlines; a pitch 'manicured' by grazing cattle from nearby Holme Farm was enclosed by a fence secured by chicken wire while the Eccleston end was simply a glorified slag heap which was somewhat incongruously dubbed 'The Spion Kop'. Nowadays only the former pavilion remains as a monument to those traumatic times.

The scoreboard was a wooden contraption emblazoned 'Saints' and 'Visitors', with metallic numbers hung on nails to indicate the score as the game progressed. A folded sheet costing tuppence masqueraded as a programme. Kit was in short supply after the war, which meant that threadbare Saints regularly issued appeals for clothing coupons.

"I well remember a game against Hunslet at Saints when our loose-forward Ernie Mills had his jersey torn from his back," said Duggie. "The club was hard-up, which meant no replacement jersey was available so we had to carry on with 12 men. However the team buckled down to earn a famous victory, and the Supporters Club made sure we had a new jersey for the following Saturday."

Rex Winter was chairman designate, Bert Murray secretary, Alf Frodsham coach and Joe Carson trainer, with Emlyn Jenkins and Peter Lyons waiting in the wings for the last two roles.

This was the austere yet hospitable Knowsley Road scenario into which an apprehensive Duggie Greenall made his grand entrance in early 1946, when his signing-on fee was the princely sum of £30 – on completion of six trial games.

He initially turned out for the 'A' team against Widnes at home, and then was sent off for a late tackle at Warrington before making his senior team debut in Saints' cliff-hanging 6-5 reverse on a wet and windy day at The Willows, Salford. The Saints line-up was: Joe Ball; Joe Helsby, Jack Bradbury, Dave Cox, Albert Doyle; Duggie Greenall, Billy French;

4

George Davies, Ike Fishwick, Nat Hornby, Johnny Jones, Frank Riley, Ernie Mills. Davies scored a try and Ball kicked a goal for Saints' points.

Greenall retained his adopted position as Frank Tracey awaited demobilisation from the Army. But when Billy French hung up his boots, and Tracey, now back in 'civvy street' moved to scrum-half, Duggie was able to revert to stand-off. However, the contrary Saints selectors juggled with the half-back combination yet again and shunted a reluctant Duggie to the wing, with captain Jim Stott - also back from military duty - as his centre.

Reflecting on those uncertain days Duggie fumed: "When my form slumped I was on the wing, then it was back to number six on regaining my magic touch. To be honest, I believe Saints were in a quandary as to where to pick me, and although they assured me my value to the team was in no doubt it was all very frustrating."

By now the durable Duggie was settling in nicely with his new team-mates at Knowsley Road, and these immediate post-war heroes at the club included Jonty Pilkington, Albert 'Sonny' Doyle, Jack Fearnley, Jim and Tom Stott, Jack Bradbury, George 'Porky' Davies, Glan Jones, Len Aston, Ike and Bill Fishwick, Albert Butler, Ray Huyton, Harry Pimblett, Jack Waring and Elwyn Bowen.

Always one for keeping in touch with former team-mates, in May 2006 Duggie paid a nostalgic visit to see Pimblett in St Helens Hospital, who had had his right leg amputated due to gangrene. Now 86, a former Welsh Guardsman and prisoner of war, Harry played full-back for Saints in the early post-war years, when Duggie was starting to make his presence felt at Knowsley Road.

Pimblett eventually joined Belle Vue Rangers with winger Stan McCormick going in the opposite direction, and Duggie recalled Harry's 45-yard drop goal at Saints in 1947, which helped Rangers to a rare victory at Knowsley Road. "Harry was appearing in his first game against Saints and when our captain Jimmy Stott cross-kicked to him on the popular side Harry let fly with the boot from the touchline, ironically with the foot he no longer has," remembered Duggie. Pimblett, incidentally, is the father of Jack, who died after being

5

injured while playing in the second row for local amateur side Pilkington Recs at City Road in the early 1970s.

Another character looming large in Duggie's memory was fiery prop Jonty Pilkington who signed for Saints on demobilisation, and succeeded Porky Davies in the number eight jersey. "I knew Jonty when he lived in Elliot Street and when he arrived at Knowsley Road his tales of service in the Irish Guards and playing as a guest at Wakefield, Batley and Castleford during the war kept everyone spellbound," recalled Duggie. "Hooker Ike Fishwick used to wind Jonty up by targeting an opponent who had just thumped him. 'Leave him to me Ike,' came the reply, and having meted out retribution the 6 feet 16 stone Pilkington usually found himself in bother with the referee. I am convinced that, with the right handling, Jonty could have been an international because he always held his own with Frank Whitcombe of Bradford and Ken Gee of Wigan. The tougher the opposition the more Pilkington liked it, and he was a good man to have on your side. "The Saints players gave him a rousing farewell when he left for Oldham in 1948, and he said he would be back at Knowsley Road with the Roughyeds. True to type, he marked his return by being sent off for flattening Dick Jones, whom Saints had bought to replace him," added Duggie.

Pilkington was also a fairground fighter, and regularly fought at Silcock's boxing booth at the Bank Holiday fair on Saints' training pitch and Queen's Recreation Park. Jonty's three-round bouts with local boxing hero Billy Beech drew large crowds, and Greenall acted as his second. "He would slip me a bob or two, but only if he won," chuckled Duggie.

Duggie's anecdotes abounded about Pilkington even after he left Saints for Watersheddings in 1948. The Roughyeds and Saints were both playing in Yorkshire and Jonty hitched a lift on the Saints coach to Huddersfield, while Jim Stott's team carried on to Dewsbury.

"Don't forget to pick me up on the way back," declared Jonty to his best pal Greenall, who immediately told the rumbustuous prop that this was not possible because Oldham's match kicked off an hour later than Saints.

"Not to worry," retorted Pilkington, "because I'll get sent off in the first half and you can rest assured that I'll be on that homebound bus" and Jonty was as good as his word.

2. Duggie on the wing

Despite emerging unscathed from his six-match baptism at stand-off, Duggie was selected on the wing on 27 occasions during the following season's campaign, when he raced over for 14 tries.

Saints had started the 1946-47 season in disastrous fashion by losing six consecutive matches, with possession – or rather lack of it - being the main problem due to Ike Fishwick being injured. Saints moved quickly to sign Italian-born Vincenzo Dilorenzo from Bradford Northern.

"And it did the trick," remembered Duggie, "because Saints won three games on the trot and morale was boosted both at the club and in the glass town in general. We had another good reason to be thankful to 'Dillo' because he worked at Crosfields in Warrington, which was known as 'Joe Soap's,' and after training he would dish out free samples of Rinso powder, Lifebuoy soap and various other exotic toiletries."

In this testing time Duggie had run himself legless in a bid to stop the rot, and it was a standing joke around St Helens and at Knowsley Road that when any supporter inquired as to what was the team for Saturday, the stock reply was "Duggie and twelve others."

Another oft-repeated tale at that time concerned Len Aston, whose mother incidentally ran a chip shop in Doulton Street, just a drop-kick from Saints' ground. Len had enjoyed a meteoric rise to test match fame, but he also made his name in an incident which was chewed over in local watering holes for many a year. For Aston was ruled by referee Paul Cowell to have made a forward pass when Saints were playing Barrow at Knowsley Road - but he had not released the ball.

"I can vouch for that," said Duggie. "Aston had a very convincing dummy that fooled everybody except me that day, because if Len had passed the ball I would have scored under the posts. Also at that time we had some real speed merchants at Knowsley Road, including household names like 'Sonny' Doyle, Eddie Cheetham and Stan McCormick, all of whom could catch pigeons. As indeed could Ernie Large who was known as the fastest milkman in town. Local lad Ernie did not stay long at Saints, but I remember playing centre to him at Hull KR and he left me in no doubt as to why he was invited to run in the Powderhall Sprint athletics competition in Edinburgh."

The winter of 1947 was a severe one indeed, with the season being extended until June because of postponed matches and restrictions on paying midweek fixtures, but for the freezing Saints' squad training was made more bearable by the prospect of then devouring mouth-watering pies and sausage rolls straight from the oven, which were brought to Knowsley Road by Lee and Devanney's of Eldon Street. "I knew the delivery girls Maureen Marren and Edna Appleton, and they used to slip me a couple of meat-and-spud pies for my supper," chuckled the irrepressible Duggie.

Probably the highlight of 1946-47, which was Duggie's initial full season in professional rugby league, was Saints' 12-7 victory at Wigan on Good Friday, their first after hitting the Billinge Lump trail since the early 1930s.

Harry Pimblett and Tommy Leyland touched down for Saints, with Jim Stott kicking two goals and Johnny Jones one. Leyland, incidentally, had to retire at half-time after breaking his collar bone, and when it is remembered that there were no substitutes in those far-away days, Saints' win was all the more praiseworthy.

On his first venture onto the hallowed Central Park turf Duggie earned this glowing media accolade: "Although not figuring in his favourite centre spot the slenderly-built, raw-boned winger Greenall lacked nothing in guts and determination, along with an ability to time both telling pass and crushing tackle that bordered on the uncanny." And that was from the Wigan local paper.

Saints line-up on that red-letter day at Central Park was: Harry Pimblett; Duggie Greenall, Tom Stott, Jim Stott, Ernie Mills; Len Constance, Glan Jones; Wally Norris, Ike Fishwick, Danny Roughsedge, Tommy Leyland, Howard Lewis, Jack Dixon.

Duggie's first brush with international opposition came at the start of the next season, 1947-48, when New Zealand opened their tour with an 11-5 triumph at Knowsley Road on Thursday 25 September, with 20,000 fans cramming into the ground.

Incidentally, the game was a repeat performance of the Kiwis' opener in 1939, a trip curtailed after just one more fixture at Dewsbury due to the outbreak of the Second World War.

Albert Doyle scored Saints' lone try following a brilliant passing movement in which the 20-year-old Duggie had a leading role. Tom Stott landed the conversion, while Len Aston caught the eyes of the Great Britain selectors to pick up his first test cap a fortnight later. The teams were:

St Helens: Eric Frodsham; Duggie Greenall, Tom Stott, Jim Stott (capt.), Albert Doyle; Len Constance, Steve Morris; Wally Norris, Reg Blakemore, Joe Aspinall, Len Aston, Tommy Heaton, Jack Dixon.

New Zealand: S. W. Clarke; A. J. McInnarney, L. R. Jordan, M. W. Robertson, R. G. McGregor; A. H. Graham, J. S. Haig; P. A. Smith (captain), W. G. Davidson, J. J. Johnson, C. McBride, J. Newton, T. H. Hardwick.

Hardwick, McGregor and Robertson scored tries for New Zealand, with Clarke kicking a goal.

Duggie's explosive arrival on the Knowsley Road scene led to after-match gatherings of admirers at the family home in Dunriding Lane, and with dad and Duggie both fond of a flutter bookmakers Bob Collins, Harry Ormesher and Bill 'Spec' Appleton were often to be found among the assembled company, as was Jack Leach, who lost a leg on the Somme in 1916.

Another visitor, by way of variation, was fish merchant Alf Critchley and his brother Cecil, with their business slogan of 'if it swims Alf's got it' occupying pride of place on Saints' makeshift scoreboard. Reliving those heady days of bonhomie and good cheer at Number 85 Duggie recalls: "The air was thick with cigar smoke and the odd noggin went down the hatch, I can tell you. I used to call this well-known clientele the St Helens Mafia."

These were also the days when Saints' director Lionel Swift, a local baker dubbed 'the jolly miller', would often dangle the carrot of a boosted winning bonus out of his own pocket if the team was struggling at half-time. He would pop his head round the dressing room door and bellow "There's 10 bob (50p) in it for you lads if Saints' win" - and it often did the trick.

Another amusing incident involving Duggie occurred at the official opening of Leigh's Hilton Park in August 1947, when Saints won a first-round Lancashire Cup match 15-0.

Due to his fallen arches problem Duggie always wore odd-sized boots. The right one was size eight and the left size nine. However, because of a misunderstanding, Duggie's footwear ended up on the feet of Len Aston, who promptly played a blinder. As for Duggie he was shunted out onto the wing because Aston's boots - which were both size 8 - were killing him.

It certainly wasn't a happy new season for the lad from Triplex. On the following Saturday and once more playing Leigh but this time at Knowsley Road, Duggie collided with a goalpost and the cone at its top fell 30 feet and hit him on the head.

Duggie explained, recalling his groggy state: "Posts were not protected in those days and the impact left me a little dazed, but trainer Joe Carson's magic sponge soon had me back on my feet. However, I gave goalposts a wide berth from then on."

In those days captain Jim Stott's warriors' kit was kept well-scrubbed courtesy of an ancient water boiler, dolly tub, rubbing board, mangle, bottle of Sallywhite, and good old-fashioned elbow grease, the latter being provided by Duggie's mum plus a team of volunteers housed in a ramshackle boot room which doubled as a launderette.

Although enforced versatility had been Duggie's lot, he stuck to his guns in the unswerving belief that centre was his best position. His persistence had its reward in 1948 when he was firmly established in his favourite number three jersey.

Little was he – or anyone else for that matter - to know at this juncture that he was destined for greatness along with the love-hate relationships that are often synonymous with partisan home and opposition supporters.

Earlier in the year Saints had signed Welsh forward George Parsons from Newport and his fellow 'Taff' Steve Llewellyn from Abertillery. 'Llew', as he became popularly known, was soon to forge a right flank partnership with Duggie that is etched indelibly into Knowsley Road folklore.

Duggie was handed the key of the door of 85, Dunriding Lane on coming of age on 7 June 1948, and by now was

10

mainly pre-occupied with arrangements for the biggest match of his life, which was looming on the immediate horizon.

For Duggie had wooed and won the hand in marriage of petite dark-haired Vera Campbell, a Sutton lass from the Pudding Bag area who, like her beau, worked at the Triplex plant at Eccleston. Let the gallant Greenall take up the romantic, if somewhat bizarre story, of their first careless rapture: "Vera had fallen off her bike outside the factory and, being a gentleman, I rushed to her aid to ensure that she was not injured. She assured me she was OK so I then chatted her up."

The parish records at Christ Church, Eccleston confirm that the vivacious Vera was so swept off her feet by the dashing Duggie that she became Mrs Greenall on Saturday - of all days - 25 September 1948, with Len Aston deputising for Duggie at Dewsbury's Crown Flatt ground, where Saints won 14-7.

"How can you forget your wedding day?" chuckled Duggie, looking back. "There were a lot of Saints' supporters in church to see me and our 'Ve'," as Duggie fondly dubbed her, "tie the marital knot.

"We held our reception at Wassell's cafe on Knowsley Road, just behind Saints' main stand, before leaving by train for our honeymoon hideaway near the Golden Mile, in Blackpool.

"However, despite Saints being on a winning streak I knew they needed me," declared Duggie modestly. "So I was back in the side the following week, although at stand-off due to an injury to Jimmy Honey. The break must have done me some good because I had a blinder as Saints' thrashed Hunslet 41-11."

On returning from Blackpool the newlyweds settled down to nuptial bliss in their own house at 28 Crowther Street which, like Dunriding Lane, is just a stone's throw from the Saints' ground.

The big-hearted club forwarded Duggie a £500 windfall both as a start to married life and to help buy the terraced property. However there seemed to be some misunderstanding regarding the financial transaction with the grateful Duggie believing it was a gift. Subsequent events proved otherwise. "I was delighted when chairman Rex

Wedded bliss! Vera and Duggie Greenall on their honeymoon
in Blackpool in 1948.

Winter called me into the boardroom to tell me that his directors had decided to help me," said Duggie, "And I could have sworn he said the money was mine for keeps but I had nothing in writing." It was a remarkable state of affairs to say the least.

As a matter of record the remainder of the Saints' directors who came to Duggie's assistance in 1948 comprised Albert Owen, Harry Cook, Cecil Dromgoole, Leslie Fairclough (a Lions tourist in 1928), Bob Lawson, George Marsden, Jim Marshall, Arthur Naylor, Lionel Swift, Jim Robinson and brothers Frank and Jim Yearsley.

Comings and goings continued unabated at Knowsley Road as Saints sought to improve on their eighth position in the previous campaign. Homespun forwards Jonty Pilkington and Tommy Leyland hit the Watersheddings trail to Oldham, while legendary prop of the future Alan Prescott came in the opposite direction from Halifax, as did Australian winger Len Kenny from Leeds.

Nonetheless, neither appeared in what was arguably Saints' best performance of the season when the mighty Australians were defeated 10-8 on a wet and windy October night, with the kick-off being put back to 4.30pm for the benefit of morning shift workers in the 20,000 crowd.

12

Once again the dauntless Duggie was to the fore when, following a brilliant break by skipper Jim Stott, he aquaplaned over the try-line and, although Tom Stott's conversion rebounded from an upright, Saints led 3-2 at half-time, with Johnny Graves landing Australia's penalty goal.

A superb 50-yard try by Clock Face-born winger Mick Lawrence, engineered by Howard Lewis and Duggie, was the highlight of the second period, during which Nevyl Hand and Les Cowie touched down for the Kangaroos. Cowie's try came in the 77th minute, and Graves missed the crucial conversion.

This was Duggie's baptismal confrontation with the awesome Australians, and Saints' first win over them in 40 years. Football maestro Stanley Matthews was among the enthralled throng on the terraces in a game refereed by St Helens' schoolmaster Norman Railton.

The teams were:

St Helens: Jimmy Lowe; Steve Llewellyn, Duggie Greenall, Jim Stott, Mick Lawrence; Len Constance, Joe Ball; Howard Lewis, Reg Blakemore, Joe Aspinall, Jack Grundy, George Parsons, Tom Stott.

Australia: V. Bulgin; R. Dimond, J. Hawke, L. Pegg, J. Graves; W. Thompson, W. O'Connell (capt.); E. Brosnan, N. Hand, J. Holland, D. Hall, J. Rayner, L. Cowie.

Optimism abounded with the dawn of the 1949-1950 season with the signing of test winger Stan McCormick from Belle Vue Rangers for a record £4,000 fee. Both first and 'A' team gates were on the increase as rugby league recovered from the drought which affected every sport in the dark days of the 1939-45 conflict.

The Saints' Supporters Club were always ready to help with cash for ground improvements, including levelling and re-seeding of the pitch. A concrete wall was added to enclose the arena while terracing of the Eccleston end was in full swing.

Former Widnes trainer Peter Lyons replaced the long-serving Alf Frodsham and, as the youngest Regimental Sergeant Major in the Army, immediately made his presence felt as a man who did not suffer fools gladly after he quickly imposed blanket discipline on his charges at Knowsley Road.

Despite the authoritarian Peter one Saint in particular refused to toe the line on certain training nights although he

St Helens versus Warrington team sheet from 1948. Duggie Greenall is on the right wing, Warrington's right winger is Brian Bevan. (Courtesy St Helens RLFC)

lived on the Knowsley Road doorstep, and that was Duggie Greenall.

"It was like this," said Duggie, "I did not like missing my favourite radio programmes such as *Dick Barton Special Agent* plus *The Man in Black* starring Valentine Dyall. And I don't mind admitting I skipped the odd training session when *Flash Gordon* was on the silver screen at the Palladium cinema in Boundary Road.

"All this tended to get me into hot water with Lyons, because he refused to start training until every player was present. He hauled me before the board on more than one occasion, but I was only a stripling of a lad and told the directors that I liked other forms of entertainment as well as rugby league.

"But at the end of the day he was right to demand rigid discipline from the Saints' players. I always had the greatest respect for Peter Lyons, both as a man and a trainer and we remained good friends until he left Saints," added the repentant Duggie.

However, despite the upsurge in their fortunes, Saints' last piece of silverware had been placed on the Knowsley Road sideboard as long ago as 1932, with the Championship success over Huddersfield at Belle Vue, Wakefield. Fans were understandably hungry for a first-ever Challenge Cup triumph. Instead, in 1949, they were about to embark on a run of three successive dismissals at the hands of Bradford Northern, twice in the first round in those days played over two legs and once in the third round in 1950, after a 0-0 draw at Knowsley Road. In these six games Duggie picked up winning money in only one of them.

"And Saints failed to score a try in all six clashes, such was the 'they shall not pass' approach of the Northern defence," reflected a rueful Duggie. "Bradford had a massive pack which included the likes of 18-stone Frank Whitcombe, Trevor Foster, Barry Tyler and Ken Traill, and although the way they kept coming down the middle was not much fun for the spectator it was certainly effective."

The details of the triple nightmare for sorry Saints were:
1948-49: 1st round: Bradford 3 Saints 4, Saints 0 Bradford 5;
1949-50: 3rd round Saints 0 Bradford 0, Bradford 11 Saints 0;
1950-51: 1st round: Bradford 11 Saints 6; Saints 4 Bradford 0.

Smarting Saints had to wait until the 1953-54 season for revenge with a 19-14 success in the league at Odsal in which captain Greenall scored two tries, and the team followed this with a 22-12 victory in the return match at Knowsley Road, with Duggie again among the try-scorers in a virtuoso personal performance.

The shadow that had been cast over Saints by Bradford was finally lifted completely with a Challenge Cup third round 53-6 drubbing of Northern at Knowsley Road in 1956, before Saints went on to a 13-2 first-ever Wembley success at the expense of Halifax.

But all that was in the future because back in 1949, the birth of Duggie junior was another cause for joy in the Greenall household, while on the field the shrewd signings of Widnesian Bill Whittaker and Warrington-born Wally Norris helped rid Saints' pack of the ill-deserved 'easy six' and 'hand-rags' tags.

Welsh rugby union signings George Parsons and Steve Llewellyn were well established in the Saints' ranks by now, after understandably taking their time in finding their feet in the XIII-a-side code. Duggie recalls: "Being a forward, Parsons found the transition easier but Llewellyn found the switch a struggle at first. Indeed his fellow Welshman and stand-off Len Constance advised Steve to forget about rugby league and go back to the Valleys after he and Parsons made a joint debut in a 9-8 defeat by Rochdale Hornets at Knowsley Road.

"However they proved the doubters wrong and played significant roles in Saints' success story before they left the club in 1957. By this time 'Llew' had scored 240 tries in 287 games and I was his centre for the majority of them."

Llewellyn twice scored six tries in a single match, against Castleford and Liverpool City in 1956 - a feat later equalled by Tom van Vollenhoven against Wakefield Trinity in 1957 and Blackpool Borough in 1967, Frank Myler and Shane Cooper. It is still a club record today.

Duggie became Saints' youngest captain at just 22 in 1949, but had to sit out the 15-8 win over Wigan on Boxing Day at Knowsley Road, when a record 35,695 crowd packed the ground to the rafters. "And that was only an estimate," reflected a nostalgic Duggie, "Because the police ordered the gates at the Eccleston end to be opened 10 minutes after kick-off because of the possibility of a crowd disaster.

"As for my shoulder injury, that was just one of a catalogue of knocks that plagued me at the time. In fact my workmates at Triplex never knew what to expect when I clocked in on Monday morning. So much so they christened me 'the bionic man'.

Eric Latham first watched Saints at the age of six in 1938, and by 1944 was a fanatical supporter who later became a director and then club chairman. He said: "During the Second World War the team consisted of mainly young local players and outstanding among them was Duggie Greenall. He was a talented centre in every respect, with his greatest attribute being tremendous defensive ability.

"Although only slightly built he tackled with the accuracy and ferocity of a player twice his size. For this daunting asset alone he earned a reputation of esteem in this country and also in Australia when on tour in 1954 with the British Lions. His partnerships with Steve Llewellyn and Tom van Vollenhoven produced an abundance of tries that has never been equalled at Saints. For the past 20 years I have been privileged to have been a close friend of Duggie through the Past Players Association. He is still as dedicated to Saints as he was in his playing days, and enjoys great popularity with colleagues past and present within the game of rugby league. He played 489 matches for Saints, and I cannot imagine any player in the current game achieving anything near this figure. His service to the club is unique and he deserves a very special place in our hearts."

St Helens in a 1947 public trial match - in orange & brown hooped jerseys
Back: left to right: Walter Norris, Jimmy Myers, Len Aston,
Ike Fishwick, Howard Lewis, Jack Dixon, Jonty Pilkington, Tommy Stott.
Front: Albert Doyle, Jimmy Stott (captain), Duggie Greenall,
Eric Frodsham, Steve Morris.

Joe Ball – Duggie Greenall's 'Siamese twin.'

Duggie Greenall takes centre stage with Len Aston as Saints are thrown onto the defensive at Naughton Park, Widnes in 1947.

St Helens in 1948:
Back, left to right. Rex Winter (chairman), Jack Grundy, Howard Lewis, George Parsons, Jimmy Lowe, Alf Frodsham (coach), Joe Aspinall, Tommy Stott, Ike Fishwick, Albert Owen (vice-chairman).
Front: Steve Llewellyn, Duggie Greenall, Jimmy Stott (captain), Mick Lawrence, Len Constance, Joe Ball.

St Helens in 1949:
Back, left to right: Steve Llewellyn, Reg Blakemore, Walter Norris,
Bill Whittaker, Jack Grundy, Alan Prescott, Len Aston.
Front: Bill Finnan, Jimmy Lowe, Stan McCormick, Duggie Greenall.
Kneeling: Jimmy Honey, Billy Holland.

Duggie Greenall races over the try-line against Swinton at Knowsley Road
in 1950, Steve Llewellyn is in the background.

Huddersfield's Pat Devery moves in to challenge Duggie Greenall at
Knowsley Road in 1952.

3. The early 1950s

The dawn of a new decade heralded the arrival of a further clutch of Welshmen at Saints. These were centres Vivian Harrison from London Welsh, plus Don Gullick and back-rower Ray Cale, who were both from Pontypool.

However, there was little cause for celebration for injury-prone Duggie in 1950 thanks to a broken jaw sustained at Leeds that meant a diet of soup and porridge and drinking through a straw for a long period.

When he recovered Duggie bounced back into the Saints side, but at stand-off in place of the departed Eric Hesketh for the 1950-51 season. But he then suffered a slump in form and was convinced that he was to be dropped, particularly following a nightmare 80 minutes at Oldham.

Wiser counsel prevailed among the Saints board however, and he was included in the squad for the home match against Barrow - but back in his favourite spot at centre. Granite-hard Duggie had a blinder.

In April 1951 Duggie was awarded a testimonial game against Halifax and, at just 24, became the youngest beneficiary in Saints' history, and had appeared in more matches than anyone else in the current squad. Gate receipts for Duggie's benefit were £900 - but the loyal clubman's joy was tempered when secretary Bert Murray told him that Saints' would deduct from this the £500 they had loaned him on his marriage.

Duggie has many other memories from these times. Another amusing tale in his colourful life occurred in the early 1950s when Duggie, along with Stan McCormick, stayed overnight at a hotel in Keswick after playing in a county match at Workington.

Duggie suddenly developed earache and, with no medical aid around, Stan suggested pouring a hot rum into the painful organ, to which the groaning Duggie readily agreed. He was a lot better the following morning and went to hospital to have the ear syringed. His dumbfounded doctor exclaimed: "Good God Mr Greenall, you must have had a skinful last night, it's coming out of your ears."

St Helens in 'civvies' at Knowsley Road in 1950. Back, left to right: Jimmy Honey, Reg Blakemore, Doug Holland, Duggie Greenall. Middle: Peter Lyons (trainer), Ray Cale, Vivian Harrison, Don Gullick, Tommy Stott, George Parsons, Bill Whittaker, Steve Llewellyn, Max Garbler, Harry Cook (chairman). Front: George Parr, Jimmy Lowe, Alan Prescott, Len Aston, Jimmy Stott, Stan McCormick, Emlyn Jenkins (coach), Joe Ball.

Around this time Duggie's loyalty to Saints was put to the test when, with Joe Ball and Billy Holland injured, the selectors were struggling to find a scrum-half for the daunting trip to Huddersfield. Centre Duggie was out with a damaged shoulder but, undeterred, Saints chairman Harry Cook and secretary Bert Murray knocked on his door and begged him to turn out at number seven at Fartown.

"But I'm drawing sick money," protested the transparently honest Duggie. "I'll be for the high jump if the authorities find out," he added. "There's not much chance of that," replied Harry Cook. "Just feed the scrum, don't run with the ball or tackle, and generally keep out of the way."

However, such well-intentioned advice was totally alien to Duggie's devil-may-care approach to the rigours of rugby league football and, with Reg Blakemore winning the first scrum, Duggie shot between the posts to give Saints an early lead, but was demolished as he touched down by Huddersfield forwards Dave Valentine and Ike Owens.

Despite the agony of aggravating his shoulder injury Duggie gamely battled on after moving to the wing with Stan McCormick switching to scrum-half. Facing such odds Saints slumped to a 19-9 defeat, with their other six points coming from the boot of former rugby union centre Vivian Harrison.

Then it was time for in-the-wars Duggie to count the cost of his commitment to his beloved Saints for, as well as the physical trauma, there was no pay from his employers Triplex and his sickness benefit was stopped, while losing money of £3 from Saints was hardly designed to keep the wolf from the door of 28, Crowther Street.

"Somebody suggested a whip-round for me on the bus as Saints made their way back home," chuckled Duggie. "You certainly discover who your friends are in a situation like this because there were few takers, although Walter Norris and George Parsons lent me a few bob so that I could take Vera to the pictures followed by chips and fish at Dickie Glover's in Corporation Street - happy days indeed."

Now established at centre, Duggie was a surprise selection for Great Britain in the first test against the New Zealand tourists on 6 October 1951.

So while Duggie and Saints could not seem to decide which position best suited him, the Rugby Football League made the choice for them and settled his position once and for all. From that moment on, except for rare occasions, Duggie was a fixture in the centre.

But conversely, the Lancashire selectors were not in a similar frame of mind as their test counterparts, for Greenall was not even included in the shadow squad for the county team chosen in the same week.

However, he played so well in the first two tests against New Zealand that Lancashire would ignore him at their peril, and Duggie eventually got the county vote. But he was also named in the England team to play France in the European Championship, and, with the two matches due to be played within four days of each other, he had to miss out on the Lancashire honour. However, his England debut did not go well, with a 42-13 defeat in Marseilles.

Rarely spectacular, but the stuff of which winning teams are made, Duggie's strengths were earth-shattering tackling and uncanny timing of a pass and he was in buoyant mood when the first test against New Zealand arrived at Odsal.

His selection did not meet with unanimous approval, indeed one national journalist said he could name half a dozen centres who would be better choices than Duggie. Furthermore, he caustically remarked that the Great Britain debutant had a face like an Ordnance Survey map, while his limbs were bent and twisted like an old oak tree. Duggie's dynamic entry onto the test scene caused the scathing scribe to eat his words and publish a complimentary headline which read "Ugly duckling turns into a Swan".

The tourists reputedly had a tough man of their own, Tommy Baxter, who quickly took the liberty of a man-and-ball demolition act on Duggie. When Duggie got to his feet he took a long, hard look at the intrepid Baxter - retribution was at hand.

And it arrived just minutes later as a wary Baxter took the ball on the burst, only to be handed a devastating dose of his own medicine as Duggie torpedoed the Kiwi, causing him to lose possession from the shuddering impact of the tackle. Visually more of a greyhound than a Goliath, Greenall had certainly made his presence felt.

Later in the game, prop Elwyn Gwyther fed Duggie inside his own half, and the Knowsley Road cult figure broke a couple of tackles before dispatching a dream of a pass to Huddersfield winger Dick Cracknell who touched down unopposed.

The irrepressible Duggie was also among the try-scorers, while his sublime skills paved the way for a debut hat-trick by his winger George Wilson of Workington. Wigan's legendary front rower Ken Gee kicked three goals as Great Britain got the three-match series of to a winning start. So, as at club level, Duggie's test career had enjoyed an auspicious baptism. The teams were:

Great Britain: J. Cunliffe (Wigan); R. Cracknell (Huddersfield), D. Greenall (St Helens), E. Ward (Bradford N), G. Wilson (Workington); R. Williams (Leeds), A. Burnell (Hunslet); K. Gee (Wigan), V. McKeating (Workington T), E. Gwyther (Belle Vue Rangers), R. Ryan (Warrington), C. Thompson (Hunslet), W. Blan (Wigan).

New Zealand: D.H. White; W. B. K. Hough; T. O. Baxter; M. Robertson, C.A. Eastlake; G. Menzies, J. S. Haig; C. R. Johnson, W. G. Davidson, W. R. McLennan, C. McBride, F. G. Mulcare, A. J. Atkinson.

The home side clinched the series with a nail-biting 20-19 victory at Station Road, Swinton, and here again Duggie got the better of his on-going confrontation with the equally belligerent Baxter. Brilliant breaks by Greenall again led to tries by wingers Cracknell and Wilson, while hooker Vince McKeating and Bradford's Ken Traill also figured among the touchdowns.

Four goals from Leigh full-back Jimmy Ledgard proved crucial in such a tight finish - a struggle that marked the debut of Duggie's club-mate Alan Prescott in what was the first-ever televised test match.

Duggie went on to play in all three tests in his initial season in representative rugby, as Great Britain completed a notable hat-trick versus New Zealand by virtue of a 16-12 success at Headingley.

However, it had been a rather different story when the smarting Kiwis came to Knowsley Road, where they trounced sorry Saints 33-10. Battle-scarred Duggie was missing from the home line-up due a damaged shoulder sustained in the first test, and Saints' tale of woe was compounded when free-scoring winger Steve Llewellyn broke his collarbone.

Overall, the Saints side bore a somewhat makeshift look, with Duggie recalling that teenage stand-off John 'Todder' Dickinson, hooker Reg Blakemore and centre Don Gullick also missed the match. Shorthanded Saints also fielded a debutant winger in Welshman Russell Dobbs.

But Duggie had a price to pay for the eventful campaign of 1951-52, because a lethal cocktail of international calls and niggling injuries meant that he figured in just 14 of Saints' 42 matches. However, the now revered Duggie nevertheless managed to score in eight of them.

And, despite the persuasive skills of chairman Harry Cook in enticing scrum-half and robotic goalkicker George Langfield from Castleford, out-of-sorts Saints plummeted to 20th in the league - their lowest place since the end of the Second World War.

A seemingly endless fixture pile-up, plus the bodily wear-and-tear of playing personnel conspired to find Saints badly in need of a break from the weekly treadmill. So a spot of 'French leave' – namely a short tour across the Channel - was to be the remedy for all ills - or so captain Duggie and his battle-fatigued troops believed.

Shell-shocked Saints were in for a rude awakening however, for they were humiliated 35-5 in the opening game at Toulouse under floodlights. Worse to follow as a French Select squad romped to a 45-5 victory at Tarascon, with prop-turned-winger Alan Prescott notching Saints' only try.

A vestige of pride was restored when the men from Knowsley Road scraped home by 27-24 at Figeac, on a day when the visitors left convinced that the home referee allowed play to run a full 15 minutes over time, in the hope that Tarascon might belatedly turn the tables on a Saints' side desperate not to return to England empty-handed.

"Some bloody holiday," protested Duggie. "With Don Gullick and Viv Harrison being unfit to travel I had to turn out in three games within five days. And with the French certainly knowing how to hand it out, we all finished up bruised and battered. It did not help that no one in the Saints party could speak French, including Harry Cook who was a headmaster, so that meant it was absolute bedlam due to the language problems.

"Add to all that the fact that our plane hit turbulence over the Pyrenees - both ways - which left most of the team and officials scared stiff; what little ale we had tasted like vinegar and it was a relief when what French currency we had ran out, so we had to sup pop. Was it any wonder that the dispirited Saints' team felt that what had promised to be a welcome jaunt developed into a French farce, and we all cheered when the plane touched down at Manchester."

Little were ambitious Saints, captain courageous Duggie and their loyal fans to know that their beloved team now stood at the threshold of a Golden Age, with Harry Cook playing his trump card in luring charismatic coach Jim Sullivan from high-flying Wigan to Knowsley Road in June 1952.

4. Jim Sullivan arrives

Silverware had been conspicuous by its absence since the Championship triumph over Huddersfield in 1932, and with the inspirational Duggie - who was to appear in 45 of the 50 games — as skipper, the omens were good for the 1952-3 season and it seemed that the cupboard would not remain bare for much longer.

Welsh full-back Jim Sullivan had spent an incredible 25 years at Wigan as player before being appointed manager-coach at Central Park in 1945-46, and had a vital role in keeping the Cherry and Whites among the major trophies for the next seven years.

On an individual note 'Sully's' soaring pedigree confirmed that Saints' resourceful chairman Cook and his board had every reason to congratulate themselves on landing a very big fish as their coach indeed.

Signed from Welsh Rugby Union in 1921, Sullivan played for Great Britain in 15 Tests, kicked a record 2,859 goals, captained Wigan when they beat Dewsbury in the first Wembley Final in 1929, and hung up his boots at Mount Pleasant, Batley, in 1946.

Legendary Jim was nudging 50 when he arrived at Knowsley Road and his defection from Saints' old enemy was the biggest bombshell to hit rugby league for years, while many dyed-in-the-wool Wiganers saw it as an act tantamount to treason.

He settled in as Saints' first ever full-time manager-coach on a seven-year contract, plus bonus payments for silverware. As captain, Duggie was the first Saints player to be introduced to the great man, and was immediately in awe of him: "He shook my hand, told me he was looking forward to meeting the team and, tongue-in-cheek, made it clear that Saints had to beat Wigan on Boxing Day.

"But that was for the future, and once we got down to the business of training Sullivan revealed himself to be a hard taskmaster who did not suffer fools gladly. Practice sessions took place behind closed doors and all players wore running pumps on the cinder track, as Saints strove to reach the same fitness levels that Jim demanded at Wigan.

"Attendance at training was compulsory with only valid reasons for absence being considered. He reminded me that no *Dick Barton* excuses would be entertained, and was adamant that he had the final say in matters of team selection.

"However, and as expected, he was a motivator *par excellence* with remarkable man-management skills, and although he was often determined to get his own way he worked wonders in matters of team spirit and in fostering good relations between the directors and players.

"Sullivan was also a firm believer in developing local talent, and with Saints' first team and 'A' team training separately, would often invite excited reserves to join the senior squad on the main pitch, with groundsmen Walter Groves and Jack Bradbury acting as messenger boys to give them the news."

Jim Sullivan's arrival at Knowsley Road engendered an almost messianic feeling that deliverance from the 20-year trophy drought was nigh. Indeed, following one particularly gruelling training stint, props Alan Prescott and Bill Whittaker were spotted carrying Duggie shoulder-high. Explanation was readily forthcoming: "We're practising for Wembley," was their light hearted response.

And certainly the omens were good for an initial season of success as Sully began with five wins in the opening six games, with Duggie touching down in three of them. In the wake of the upsurge following the arrival of Sullivan, Saints' players naturally wanted their slice of the cake, and when their new pay demands were turned down they hinted at strike action.

As captain Duggie had to present the team's case to chairman Harry Cook, who in turn reported to the 12-man board. Never stuck for a word, Duggie quickly reminded Harry Cook that the current rate of £8.50 for a win and £6 for a defeat at home with slightly enhanced pay away from home was now unrealistic. The payments were also subject to tax.

Saints' initial response was that, along with the capture of the coaching maestro Sullivan, the club had also invested in other signings including those of Glyn Moses from Wales and George Langfield from Castleford.

A period of delicate negotiation was brought to a harmonious conclusion when Mr Cook, who could sell ice to the Eskimos, handed Duggie a compromise package deal which was accepted by the 18-man squad. But the cagey Duggie refused to reveal the size of a pay increase awarded more than half a century ago. However, he did divulge that Saints received £15 a man when they were defeated by Huddersfield at Wembley in 1953, and £30 for the win over Halifax in the 1956 Challenge Cup Final.

Soaraway Saints also reached the Lancashire Cup semi-final, and self-belief went through the roof when the 1952 side repeated their cliff-hanging victory over Australia of four years before, but this time to the resounding tune of 26-8, in front of a crowd of 17,205.

All this was from a Saints' squad lacking the injured Steve Llewellyn, Ray Cale, George Parsons, Don Gullick and Bill Whittaker, and facing a full strength Kangaroos line-up who suffered their only defeat against a club side in 1952.

"Yet again Jim proved that tactically he had few equals on a rugby league field," outlined Duggie, "because his ability to instil a positive frame of mind before kick-off was uncanny, and he also ensured that Saints made full use of the wind with long touch-finders in the first half, when we led 21-5."

Scrum-half George Langfield was the hero of the hour with 17 points courtesy of seven goals and a try, with the other touchdowns credited to Stan McCormick with two and 'Todder' Dickinson. For Australia, Flannery and Collinson scored tries, with a goal from Pidding.

The teams were:

St Helens: Jimmy Lowe; John Dickinson, Duggie Greenall (captain), Wilf Roach, Stan McCormick; Jimmy Honey, George Langfield; Alan Prescott, Reg Blakemore, George Parr, Stan Thornett, Bill Bretherton, Vince Karalius.

Australia: C. Churchill (capt.); N. Pidding, N. Hazzard, R. Duncan, D. Flannery; C. Geelan, C. Donohue; D. Hall, K. Schubert, C. Gill, T. Tyrrell, A. Collinson, H. Crocker.

Duggie had often been at cross-purposes with his opposite number Noel Hazzard, and the bad blood this created boiled over when they clashed again just 10 days later as the Australians defeated Lancashire 36-11 at Warrington's Wilderspool stadium.

What was a torrid affair erupted into an unseemly brawl, and at the final whistle the pent-up Kangaroos singled out Duggie for special attention. Intent on self-preservation, he made a beeline for the sanctuary of the dressing room but when he arrived there, to his horror, the door was locked.

However Leigh's Charlie Pawsey came to his frantic team-mate's rescue on hearing his cries for help, as the enraged Hazzard and company raced down the tunnel seeking retribution.

A couple of weeks earlier, Duggie captained England for half a game, against Wales at Wigan, when injured skipper Willie Horne did not return in the second half. Duggie scored a try in England's 19-8 win.

Meanwhile, back with St Helens, a hard-fought 17-10 win against Warrington at Wilderspool in the Lancashire Cup semi-final meant Saints had reached their first Lancashire Cup Final since the 10-9 reverse - also against Warrington at Wigan in 1932. Skipper Duggie was mobbed by ecstatic supporters who were convinced that long wait for silverware was to be over at last, with rank outsiders Leigh standing in Saints' way in the Final.

But their joy was short lived in the Final at Swinton's Station Road. For despite warnings of complacency by coach Sullivan, sorry Saints sank into a trough of big-match nerves, typified by handling errors, powder-puff tackling and a general malaise in front of a 34,785 crowd.

Cock-a-hoop Leigh took full advantage and led 15-2 at half-time through tries by Sutton Manor product Frank Kitchen with two and Brian Chadwick, plus three goals from Jimmy Ledgard. Two of the Leythers' touchdowns were engineered by former St Helens Recs centre Teddy Kerwick who, now aged 84, still lives at Windle - just around the corner from Duggie.

With full-time looming, Don Gullick crashed over for a Saints' try that was of no more than consolation value, but even then Leigh had the last laugh when Australian centre Trevor Allen romped over for Ledgard to land his fifth goal.

This ended a day of disaster for the league leaders, the shock result once again re-affirming the long-held belief that cup rugby can be a different ball game from league matches.

Philosophical to the last, Jim Sullivan told his disappointed side: "Forget it, we'll talk about it at training on Tuesday."

As for down-in-the-mouth Duggie, he concedes that Leigh were the better side on the day and also paid tribute to his opposite number Kerwick: "Ted had a blinder," said Duggie. "Not bad for a St. Helens lad who made his debut for the 'old Recs' as long ago as 1938." The teams were:

St Helens: Jimmy Lowe; Steve Llewellyn, Duggie Greenall (capt.), Don Gullick, Stan McCormick; Jimmy Honey, George Langfield; Alan Prescott, Reg Blakemore, Bill Whittaker, George Parsons, Bill Bretherton, Ray Cale.

Leigh: Jimmy Ledgard; Brian Chadwick, Trevor Allen, Teddy Kerwick, Frank Kitchen; Ken Baxter, Tommy Bradshaw; Harry Edden, Joe Egan, Stan Owen, Charlie Pawsey, Rex Mossop, Peter Foster.

Smarting Saints did not have to wait long for revenge for they journeyed to Hilton Park on Christmas Day 1952, and trounced the home side 22-2, with full-back Glyn Moses making an impressive debut. A Welshman from Newbridge, Glyn originally signed for Salford as a centre prior to returning home disillusioned with Rugby League, before Jim Sullivan snapped him up for a bargain £800.

"Straight from the kick-off at Leigh, Moses played as though he had never been missing from the game" said Duggie. "What I remember in particular was his tremendous defence and the ability to link-up at the right moment - a future international if ever there was one," he concluded. How correct those words of wisdom were to prove.

Returning the compliment, Windle-based Glyn said of Duggie: "I first met him when I signed for Saints in December 1952. The team was enjoying a rich vein of form and he was one of the main reasons why. Duggie was the star of the Saints backs at the time; we were winning lots of matches and went to Wembley under his leadership, and picked up several other cups in the bargain.

"Duggie was chosen for the British Lions' squad that toured Australia in 1954, and rightly so because he was hitting the headlines week-in week-out. He was a great fan of Al Jolson and needed no persuading to give 'em *Mammy* – his favourite. He also liked the occasional drink or two, or three.

31

"On the field I would call him 'the Destroyer,' because he had such split-second timing he could stop a movement before it had time to develop. Gutsy Duggie was an utterly fearless tackler, although he was not a big 'un. You could say he was a man to have alongside you in the trenches.

"I had great pleasure in lining up with Duggie Greenall and had many good times with him off the field as well. He was Saints through and through and a credit to the town of St Helens," he concluded.

By the dawn of 1953 coach Sullivan had finely tuned Saints' soaring skills to something approaching the sublime, with his 'no mercy' doctrine regardless of the quality of the opposition occasionally finding Saints branded as 'baddies' - particularly when playing away. Another reason for this dubious distinction was the controversial Duggie, whose take-no-prisoners tackles scarcely endeared him to partisan home supporters.

With no pretensions to being cast in the classical mould, Duggie was nonetheless among the top centres in rugby league while in his pomp, as League leaders Saints remained undefeated away from home in 1952-53 and the team moved inexorably towards silverware at long last.

Duggie's specific *tour-de-force* was an outside swerve before drawing the opposing winger, and then displaying an uncanny sense of timing in slipping a peach of a pass to his wingman, with a try often on the cards. Despite his reputation going before him as an uncompromising roughhouse who was homespun and proud of it, Duggie was sent off just twice in his 13-season career in what is regarded as the toughest game in the sporting pantheon.

In a bid to focus on his 'Exocet missile' demolition jobs at the centre of the action it might be pertinent to paraphrase winger Steve Llewellyn, Duggie's partner in 151 matches in a lethal right flank pairing from 1948 to 1957.

Said the late Llew: "Duggie's favourite technique was to stay out close to me so that he would come in on the blind-side, so to speak. Then he would jump - that's the best way to describe it - and use his arms in bow-like fashion. Often it was his chest that hit the man and Duggie's arms would flail around him, and down they would go together. Very often the tackled player did not get up but Duggie usually did.

32

There were countless instances of opposition players being left in cloud cuckoo land, but Duggie regularly escaped without even a warning.

"When the tackle had been completed he would tell me to follow him because the ball would sometimes come adrift because of the impact of the Greenall torpedo. However I have to say that Duggie appeared to be acting within the letter of the law. Whether it would now be ruled as a dangerous tackle I am not sure but it certainly was not a clear-cut stiff arm. I remember Duggie's inimitable challenges as a leap - chest out, head up and both arms all-embracing."

Lightweight in poundage but heavyweight in performance, the likeable lad from Rivington Road School was dubbed 'Mister Muscles' by streetwise Jim Sullivan. He up-ended jumbo-sized forwards with relish. Among Duggie's most unforgettable tackles was one on Dave Valentine of Huddersfield, who was an all-in wrestler and hard man. The Scot from Hawick had possession on the best side at Knowsley Road and targeted the on-rushing Greenall, who took off in a split second. It was a classic case of an indestructible force colliding with an immovable object, or so it seemed. Down went Dave and Duggie, but only Valentine needed assistance to regain his feet and composure.

By now Duggie's talents had blossomed into a more diverse form of entertainment which was more demanding on his vocal chords than his physical prowess, for his rafter-raising impersonations of singer Al Jolson guaranteed him rave notices in pubs, clubs and other watering holes in and around St Helens.

His party piece was a resonating rendition of the American deep south spiritual *Mammy*, second only in demand by adoring audiences to George Gershwin's *Swanee*. And it is quite a coincidence that Duggie's birth year 1927 was the time that his idol Jolson appeared in his first film *The Jazz Singer*.

Inevitably when the Kangaroos came to Knowsley Road in 1952 the popular side fans took up the incessant chant of "give 'em Mammy Duggie," as Saints gave a tourist team in some disarray the run-around. But, spearheaded by skipper Clive Churchill, the chastened Australians refused to accept that a sylph-like figure such as Duggie could create havoc in the way he did that day, and were adamant that Duggie had 'armed' himself with a secret weapon - a plaster cast hidden in his right sleeve.

Duggie swore that it was nothing more than a medically approved elastoplast, but the allegation was taken seriously by the media down under, which meant that Duggie could expect a hostile reception should he tour Australia in 1954.

Warrington's Ron Ryder was preferred to Greenall for the first Test at Leeds which Great Britain won 19-6, but Duggie came back with a bang in scoring two tries when the Kangaroos were thrashed 21-5 at Swinton in the second test, and here again battle was joined by Duggie and Noel Hazzard, who suffered a broken jaw.

With the series now decided Great Britain slumped to a 27-7 defeat in the third Test at Bradford, when Duggie and Alan Prescott were included in the line-up.

Duggie was now recognised as a real character, with headlines both censorious and complimentary charting his often turbulent times on the rugby league scene, both at club and international level. However, there was a lighter side to Duggie, with anecdotes galore lacing his career from Batley to Brisbane, Halifax to Auckland and Wigan to Workington.

One typical tale was recalled by Steve Llewellyn at the Cumbrian side's Borough Park ground on a winter's day in 1952. "Saints won 22-5 with Greenall scoring four tries and kicking two goals, and I touched down for the other two," said Steve. "It was Duggie's third that I remember best, because he put in an up-and-under and charged down on full-back Gus Risman screaming 'Geronimo' at the top of his voice. Normally safe-as-houses Gus dropped the ball and Greenall snapped it up to complete his hat-trick. Referee George Phillips waved aside the Workington players' protests saying he did not hear Duggie's war-cry."

Saints remained undefeated away from home in the league that season and captain Duggie scored 29 tries, his right wing partnership alongside Steve Llewellyn added another 35 tries. It is firmly cemented as one of the most fruitful in Knowsley Road annals.

The fleet-footed pair were known on the terraces as 'Duggie and Llew' by the Saints' faithful, and enjoyed a scoring bonanza against Wakefield Trinity at Knowsley Road in March 1953 when Saints won by a record 69-17. Llewellyn touched down five times and Greenall four, with deputy goalkicker Duggie on target on four occasions with the boot. Earlier in that momentous campaign Duggie's finely tuned centre skills had much to do with a hat-trick of tries by local teenage winger Alec Davies on his debut.

High-riding in the league, Saints' silverware aspirations were also focused on a first-ever Challenge Cup triumph following the disappointments of 1897, 1915 and 1930. And they set off in style with a two-legged success over Oldham, who were a real power in rugby league in the 1950s. Duggie figured among the try scorers when the Roughyeds were defeated 20-4 at Knowsley Road, and Saints followed that up by drawing 5-5 at wintry Watersheddings.

Belle Vue Rangers were swept aside 28-0 at Knowsley Road in the second round, then Duggie's braves were embroiled in a battle royal at Hilton Park, Leigh, and emerged victorious 12-3 in a torrid encounter on a day when home skipper Joe Egan broke his leg and the crowd was a club record 31,326.

Only Warrington now stood between Saints and their first trip to Wembley since 1930, and the pre-match atmosphere was electric according to Duggie. "'No one spoke in the dressing room except Jim Sullivan," said the Saints' skipper. "And after he had plotted the Wire's downfall I well remember Sully's last words as we went down the tunnel: 'This is it lads, Wembley beckons and you owe it to yourselves and the fans to make sure Saints' get there'."

That Saints' hopes were ultimately realised is now a matter of history, but not before a titanic struggle of cliffhanging dimensions as Warrington made Saints battle every inch of the way for a 9-3 passport to the famous Twin Towers. Indeed, Warrington led 3-2 at half-time courtesy of a Brian Bevan try, while George Langfield landed Saints' penalty goal.

The second half remained pointless until the closing minutes and it seemed the Wire were poised for a shock victory until the laid back Langfield took a hand - or should it have been a boot? His angled 40-yard drop goal inched Saints into a still-tenuous 4-3 lead.

"But we could not relax even then," recalled Duggie, "because Warrington were still coming on strong at Saints, and we only started to breathe easier when Don Gullick charged down Ron Ryder's kick to score under the posts for Langfield to convert.

"Match-winner George and myself were chaired shoulder-high by Saints' ecstatic supporters and the champagne flowed like water in the dressing room but, being a strict teetotaller, I was only drinking lemonade and soda," claimed Duggie.

One ecstatic fan was inspired to compose a lilting ditty with Wembley in mind. Duggie discovered a fading, yellowing copy at home. It was sung the length and breadth of St. Helens to the tune of *Side by Side*, which was a national patriotic melody in 1953. These are the words:

Though we ain't got a barrel of money,
We've got Langfield and Honey,
Duggie and Llew, running them through,
Side by side.

Prescott, Parr and Reg Blakemore,
Parson's kick makes them work more,
Bretherton and Cale, telling the tale,
Side by side.

Through all kinds of weather,
Saints turn out to play,
We have to give them credit,
For playing Jim Sullivan's way.

Then we've got Moses and Gullick,
With Mac coming through like a bullet.
Through hail, rain or snow, to Wembley we'll go,
Side by side.

5. Wembley here we come

So, after 23 years, St Helens was in the grip of Wembley fever and the glass town was transformed virtually overnight into a sea of red and white favours, while Duggie and his warriors were thrust into instant celebrity status.

"The team was mobbed everywhere they went," remembered Duggie. "Posing for photographs, signing autographs, opening garden fêtes, kissing babies, the list was endless - you might have thought that Saints had already won the Challenge Cup. In fact, if Saints had accepted all the offers of a drink we could have been legless before we got to Wembley.

"As for being a celebrity," he continued, "I remember being invited to a Labour Club with Manchester City's Bert Trautmann, who had earlier played in goal for St Helens Town. I made a speech, gave 'em *Mammy*, and drew the raffle before a full house who gave me a standing ovation.

"All that Bert did was sit at the top table, for which he received £50 plus expenses. Me? I didn't even get my bus fare. So much for being a big name."

Such was the tidal wave of enthusiasm from Eccleston to Earlestown, Prescot to Parr, Denton's Green to Derbyshire Hill that 13 special trains and a 240-strong armada of coaches were needed to transport more than 20,000 delirious Saints fans to the Empire Stadium on Saturday 25 April in Coronation year.

That memorable year of 1953 was notable for other achievements of worldwide interest, not least the England cricket team winning the Ashes skippered by Len Hutton, football immortal Stanley Matthews earning his one Cup Final winners' medal, and the conquering of Everest by Edmund Hillary and Tenzing Norgay.

But, certainly from a rugby league supporters' perspective, the controversial events of what promised to be a showpiece Challenge Cup Final between Saints and Huddersfield were to reverberate much further than the two industrial towns for many a long year to come, with Saints finding themselves branded as 'sinners'.

Cosmopolitan 'Fartown', as Huddersfield were then known, fielded very few locally-born players while Saints boasted just three in Duggie, Jimmy Honey and George Parr. Remarkably the Knowsley Road team included six Welshmen: Glyn Moses, Steve Llewellyn, Don Gullick, George Parsons, Reg Blakemore and Ray Cale.

In Wembley week favourites Saints had prepared well for the daunting task ahead by training on the pitch at King George School in Southport, where the yielding turf was said to be similar to that at Wembley. Then it was down to London to the pre-match headquarters at the plush Selsdon Park Hotel, Croydon, where no expense was spared in ensuring that skipper Duggie's charges were fully relaxed for the biggest occasion in the rugby league calendar.

"I will never forget the deafening roar that greeted the teams as they came down the tunnel. And when I heard the constant chanting of 'give 'em Mammy Duggie' it brought a lump to my throat and tears to my eyes," recalled Duggie.

As for the game itself the opening 30 minutes were no place for the faint-hearted as both Saints and Huddersfield adopted an overtly physical approach, with the Yorkshire side's stand-off Peter Ramsden receiving a most unwelcome 19th birthday present when he broke his nose after a 6th-minute collision with the uncompromising Don Gullick.

Ramsden quickly recovered, however, and within a minute had sidestepped Jimmy Honey, Glyn Moses and Gullick, only to be superbly cover-tackled by Alan Prescott in the act of touching down. Referee George Phillips ignored Saints protests of a double movement in awarding the try, to which Australian Pat Devery added the goal. Phillips then warned Duggie that he would be the first player to be sent off at Wembley if his objections did not stop.

Television cameras were not present thanks to an RFL ruling, but subsequent newsreel footage revealed that St Helens' dissent was justified, a point taken up by Duggie at the time and he remains convinced that the try should have been disallowed.

However, shell-shocked Saints hit back with a penalty goal from George Langfield before, on the stroke of half-time, brilliant passing involving Duggie, Moses and Stan McCormick put Llewellyn over after a 60-yard run to level the scores at

5-5. Langfield missed the conversion but made amends early in the second half in putting the finishing touch to a 70-yard movement by touching down under the posts. No doubt exhausted in reaching the tryline, the player dubbed 'Golden Boot' missed the relatively easy kick.

Saints were now 8-5 up after an hour, but found themselves embroiled in dissent yet again when Huddersfield's Australian full-back Johnny Hunter was stretchered off after being tackled by Llewellyn, who was renowned for sportsmanship and fair play.

The Yorkshire side's fans were furious in condemning what they felt was an illegal challenge, but Llew's version of events made rather different reading. He said: "Hunter came up to make the extra man between Russell Pepperell and Lionel Cooper. I moved in to mark Hunter having assumed that Duggie would tackle Pepperell, who was the man in possession. But Russell dummied and I was already committed to tackling Hunter, but in no way was it of the stiff-arm variety. I knew Hunter was hurt but it was not enough to need the stretcher, certainly no more than the magic sponge. Referee Phillips had a word with me but did not award a penalty. Nevertheless I was booed every time I touched the ball from them on, while radio commentator Harry Sunderland described the unfortunate incident as 'typical Greenall' - a classic case of mistaken identity if ever there was one. As a result Sunderland was banned from Knowsley Road by chairman Harry Cook, but this was later lifted."

Consequently Huddersfield were reduced to 12 men for 10 minutes, but managed to steal into a 10-8 lead when Welsh scrum-half Billy Banks darted over for Cooper to tack on the extra points. Controversy reigned again for newsreel film proved that Banks fed the scrum when Saints should have had the put-in.

Langfield squared matters at 10-10 with a snap drop-goal in the closing minutes, before a second try from Lance Todd Trophy winner Ramsden ensured that the Challenge Cup would be placed on the sideboard at Fartown, Cooper converting his score. Meanwhile smarting Saints were left to lick their wounds following a highly-charged Final.

Naturally disconsolate, Saints then had to endure the embarrassment of being cat-called by jubilant Huddersfield fans on their way to the dressing rooms. Dignified-in-defeat Duggie did not resort to excuses but simply added that Wembley was a very lonely place to be for a team beaten by only 15-10. The teams were:

St Helens: Glyn Moses; Steve Llewellyn, Duggie Greenall (capt.), Don Gullick, Stan McCormick; Jimmy Honey, George Langfield; Alan Prescott, Reg Blakemore, George Parr, George Parsons, Bill Bretherton, Ray Cale.

Huddersfield: Johnny Hunter; Peter Henderson, Russell Pepperell (capt.), Pat Devery, Lionel Cooper; Peter Ramsden, Billy Banks; Ted Slevin, George Curran, Jim Bowden, Jack Brown, Jack Large, Dave Valentine.

Despite being somewhat muted, the post-match banquet went ahead as planned, although there was a certain amount of panic when skipper Duggie went absent without leave. He was eventually traced to the hotel ballroom where a high society debutante was holding her 21st birthday party. There was Duggie, 'mic' in hand, with the well-heeled audience spellbound as he gave 'em *Mammy* and other Al Jolson and Frank Sinatra numbers, with accompaniment provided by the evening-suited orchestra.

Sorely disappointed Saints were not relishing the homeward journey on Monday. However their fears were without foundation as thousands of loyal supporters saw Victoria Square bursting at the seams, with every vantage point taken and all police leave cancelled in the interests of public safety.

Rising to the emotion of the occasion, Duggie gave the milling throng a few more tuneful renditions from the Town Hall steps, then introduced the Saints squad, before finally vowing to bring back the League Championship trophy to St Helens in a fortnight's time. How prophetic his words were.

Just seven days after the Wembley disappointment smarting Saints faced Huddersfield again, this time in the Championship semi-final at Knowsley Road. Coincidentally this was on the same day that Stanley Matthews won his only FA Cup winner's medal when Blackpool defeated Bolton Wanderers beneath the Twin Towers.

Revenge was obviously very much in the air from a Saints side also imbued with a steely determination to reach their first Championship Final since 1932, when Huddersfield were also the opposition and the men from Knowsley Road emerged victorious by a cliff-hanging 9-5 at Belle Vue, Wakefield.

But prospects of a third nail-biter quickly evaporated, as slick-handling Saints ran riot with a 10-try eight-goal demolition job, with influential Duggie and incoming half-backs John 'Todder' Dickinson and Peter Metcalfe regularly at the hub of the scoring bonanza.

This dynamic duo replaced Wembley choices Honey and Langfield, and these were Saints' only changes, while Huddersfield thought likewise by drafting in Dick Cracknell and Jim Cooper for Pat Devery and Jack Large.

Such was Saints' superiority in front of a 30,000 crowd that they led 28-0 at half-time with two tries from Parsons, and others from Moses, McCormick, Greenall and Cale, plus five goals from former Pilkington Recs stand-off Metcalfe.

There was little let-up for the beleaguered Fartowners on the restart, as mercurial left-winger McCormick broke away to send Llewellyn swallow-diving over on the opposite flank and, at this stage, visions of a 50-point thrashing remained a distinct prospect for the Yorkshire side.

Block-busting centre Gullick then removed the hapless Hunter from his path on an unstoppable charge for Saints' eighth try. Parsons completed his hat-trick before a last-gasp touchdown by teenager Dickinson, along with three further conversions from Metcalfe, meant honour had been restored for Saints with a 46-0 triumph.

An emotion-charged dressing room heard tributes paid to the soaraway Saints, and to Welsh colossus Parsons for his three-try contribution – a rare feat for a forward then - while Jim Sullivan's rallying call to his troops for one more Herculean effort against Halifax in the Final was positively Churchillian. Captain-courageous Duggie said he felt Saints were on the threshold of something big, adding: "We didn't play Halifax this season when we finished top of the table and remained unbeaten away from home in the league. But I don't see any reason why that record should end at Maine Road, Manchester, next Saturday."

41

The 1953 Challenge Cup Final

Left: The programme from the 1953 Challenge Cup Final. (Courtesy RFL)

Below: In mufti - Wembley blazers. St Helens in 1953. Back, left to right: Ray Cale, Bill Bretherton, Steve Llewellyn, Don Gullick. George Parsons, Wilf Roach, George Parr, Alan Prescott. Middle: Bill Whittaker, Jimmy Honey, John Dickinson, Harry Cook (chairman), Duggie Greenall (captain), Jim Sullivan (coach), Stan McCormick, Vince Karalius. Front: George Langfield, Reg Blakemore, Glyn Moses.

A moment to savour!
St Helens (left) and Huddersfield enter the Wembley arena.
Chairman Harry Cook and skipper Duggie Greenall lead the Saints' line-up.

The Duke of Norfolk greets the St Helens team before the match.
The visible Saints' players are, left to right, Don Gullick, Stan McCormick,
Jimmy Honey, George Langfield, Alan Prescott, Reg Blakemore, George
Parr, George Parsons, Bill Bretherton.

Steve Llewellyn evades Huddersfield's Johnny Hunter. Duggie Greenall and Lance Todd trophy winner Peter Ramsden are in the background.

Beaten but unbowed! Skipper Duggie Greenall and his team being welcomed home at the Town Hall by Mayor Percy Griffiths after the Challenge Cup Final defeat.

6. The Championship

Could Saints beat Halifax was the $64,000 question on the lips of every Saints supporter as their heroes prepared for the ultimate league showdown against the hardy men from Thrum Hall. As at Wembley a fortnight earlier, St Helens became a ghost town when more than 20,000 red and white bedecked fans converged on the Manchester City football ground, with a gate of 51,083 testimony to the drawing power of rugby league in those pre-television days.

League leaders Saints had finished with 66 points from 36 games compared with runners up Halifax's 60, while the respective points differentials saw Saints enjoy a massive attacking advantage of 769 points to Halifax's 620, with the defensive figures being 273 points to 309 again in favour of the Knowsley Road squad.

All the indicators were that Duggie's side would keep faith with the open handling and running strategy that had paid handsome dividends up to then, while a Halifax team hoping to lift the trophy for the first time since 1907 were expected to adopt a dour forward approach.

And so it proved with Saints laying down a marker of what was to follow by scoring the opening try after just four minutes. Hooker Blakemore heeled the ball within Saints' territory before slick passing put winger Llewellyn away, and he drew Halifax full-back Tyssul Griffiths to send the supporting Blakemore over for Metcalfe to convert.

The magical Metcalfe was already exacting the maximum toll from Saints' early command of the scrums, a point quickly noted by local writer Tom Reynolds in the *St Helens Reporter*: "With sleight of hand, body swerve and turn of head, the youthful Metcalfe was leaving behind his more experienced opponent Ken Dean. In addition Peter was weaving and side-stepping his way past the cover with the assurance of a veteran, therefore creating gaps for his talented threequarters to exploit."

Metcalfe then added a penalty goal plus having a hand in two further tries, as Saints threatened to run riot in the opening quarter. Duggie put the finishing touch to the first raid, before he and Todder Dickinson split the Halifax defence for Metcalfe to touch down.

Both conversion attempts failed, but in leading 13-0 on the half hour Saints looked to be sitting pretty, only for the Thrum Hall based team to hit back with a try by former All Black Tommy Lynch, to which Griffiths duly added the goal.

By 60 minutes, resilient Halifax had reduced the deficit to just 13-9 courtesy of a brace of Griffiths penalty goals, and there was more than a hint of panic in Saints' ranks as anxious fans pondered the possibility of a change in fortunes, as in the Lancashire Cup and Wembley Finals.

However, their worst fears were quickly dispelled as Saints loose-forward Cale plunged over the line from a play-the-ball, and then the ubiquitous Blakemore sold an outrageous dummy to score, with Metcalfe tacking on the extra points.

Full-back Moses linked with the attack to put the final nail in the Halifax coffin with a try following a break by fellow Welshman Llewellyn, while Wilkinson's last-gasp touchdown, which was converted by Griffiths, was of no more than consolation value to the Yorkshiremen. The teams were:

St Helens: Glyn Moses; Steve Llewellyn, Duggie Greenall (captain), Don Gullick, Stan McCormick; Peter Metcalfe, John Dickinson; Alan Prescott, Reg Blakemore, George Parr, George Parsons, Bill Bretherton, Ray Cale.

Halifax: Tyssul Griffiths; Brian Vierod, Tommy Lynch, Martin Creeney, Terry Cook; Ken Dean, Stan Kielty; Mick Condon, Alvin Ackerley (captain), Jack Wilkinson, Albert Fearnley, Harry Greenwood, Des Clarkson.

Recent painful memories of Wembley were soon forgotten and grown men wept tears of joy - 21 years had been a long time - as conquering heroes Saints paraded the Championship trophy on the Town Hall steps for the first time since the days of the great depression in 1932.

Mayor Percy Griffiths congratulated skipper Greenall and his team, before deeply-moved Duggie said this was the happiest moment of his rugby league career. Saints' celebrated number three then put the icing on the cake for the adoring throng assembled in Victoria Square by giving 'em *Mammy*, in an ear-splitting, misty-eyed rendition of his theme song.

Saints chairman Harry Cook added that, unlike the Challenge Cup, the Championship Trophy was the reward for a season of consistency, and called for three cheers for coaching maestro Jim Sullivan, whose record of three finals and two cups in his short time at Knowsley Road spoke volumes for the commitment and know-how of the one-time Wales and Wigan legend.

Understandably, the glass town basked in the heady brew of Championship glory for several weeks in the wake of the conquest of Halifax, with skipper Duggie and his Saintly warriors being invited to all manner of celebrations.

These included parading the red-and-white-adorned trophy at hospitals, schools, garden fêtes, pubs, clubs and charity events. They even ventured into enemy territory on the other side of Billinge Lump, a historic landmark equidistant between St Helens and arch-rivals Wigan.

Bookie Bob Collins threw a lavish celebration party after Saints' Championship triumph, with the wine flowing like water well into the small hours at his Taylor Park home. The team enjoyed a heroes' welcome from Bob and his family plus a veritable 'who's who' of guests. Skipper Duggie passed the bedecked trophy to all and sundry in order to toast the victory in vintage champagne.

An evening of sheer ecstasy moved on, with the hosts, players and guests eventually retiring to their beds. But Duggie's early-morning slumber was due for a rude awakening by panic-stricken thoughts of the whereabouts of the Championship Cup.

Said Duggie: "As captain I was responsible for the cup's safety, and the last I had seen of the silverware was in Bob Collins's front lounge. So I immediately telephoned him, and was dumbstruck when he said the Cup was nowhere to be seen. An exhaustive search of the house revealed nothing, and by now desperation was setting in before someone had a brainwave and looked in the garden.

"And there were the rewards of a season's gruelling efforts, rather bedraggled and soaking wet after being out in the pouring rain all night. Needless to say, I took the somewhat tarnished trophy back to Knowsley Road in the blink of an eye, gave it a polish and made good my escape."

On an individual note there was little respite for the highly articulate Duggie, who now found himself in constant demand on the after-dinner speaking circuit along with sportsmen's evenings, when the bill of fare comprised hot-pot, mild and bitter.

The success that Saints enjoyed during that momentous campaign of 1952-53 was something of a mixed blessing in the opinion of tongue-in-cheek Duggie. "When it all ended I still tipped the scale at 11-and-a-half stone, but after a few weeks of wining and dining I had ballooned by two to three stones," he said.

"But, of course, training had been put on hold for two months and the break gave the team time to relax and take a holiday after a gruelling season when Saints played more than 40 games including cup-ties and play-offs," added Duggie, who still carries slight traces of the scars of battle.

However, what should have been a well-earned, week-long excursion to South Wales for Duggie, wife Vera, four-year-old Duggie junior, and Saints' hooker Reg Blakemore became tinged with a nightmare on-going trauma.

Duggie took up the sorry story: "We were taking Reg back to his home town of Newport in my pride-and-joy Morris Ten, and somewhere in Shropshire another motorist signalled that our car had developed a wheel wobble. I asked Blakemore to drive a few yards so that I could check which wheel was on the blink. However, although he worked for British Road Services, Reg said he did not hold a driving licence and, to be honest, neither did I.

"So we were in a right pickle, but the four of us eventually made if to Newport a trifle late, but nonetheless still in one piece and looking forward to a reunion with Blakemore's family and a sample of Welsh hospitality.

"Then disaster struck when I took my son for a little gentle run in a local park. On turning suddenly, he was knocked down by a huge Alsatian dog and suffered a broken femur, which is a tremendous shock to the system for any youngster.

"He spent six weeks in Newport Infirmary and his mum stayed close at hand, while I travelled to South Wales by train each weekend from St Helens or wherever Saints happened to be playing."

Duggie was obviously very concerned and recalled: "I boarded the wrong train one foggy night in Barrow and found myself heading for - of all places - Wigan, and consequently arrived in Newport at midnight."

Happily Duggie junior made a good recovery from what proved to be a compound fracture, although the injured leg remained marginally shorter than the other. He played a little rugby league at school, but never aspired to following his father's footsteps. His main sporting activity was golf.

Supercharged Saints began where they left off when the 1953-54 season kicked off by remaining undefeated for nine games, including a cliffhanging Lancashire Cup first round win over Barrow. The Shipbuilders won 14-13 at Craven Park before Saints inched home 21-17 at Knowsley Road in the second leg.

"It was a close-run affair," remembered Duggie, who had been an ever-present up to then. "We had to thank a late try by up-and-coming Vince Karalius for getting Saints through to round two." This brought Swinton to Knowsley Road and the Lions were well and truly tamed 38-9, and yet they held Saints to a mere 2-0 a month later in a league game on the same ground.

A bruising home triumph against Warrington ensured a mouth-watering Lancashire Cup Final with Wigan at Station Road, Swinton, which was – incredibly - the first-ever cup final in any competition between the arch-rivals.

As its name suggests the time-honoured stadium stood next to the busy rail terminal, and special trains ferried thousands of fans from St Helens and Wigan, with both sets of supporters seizing the opportunity to engage in the usual good-humoured pre-match banter. The East Lancashire Road was also awash with rugby league traffic, with the net result being a competition record crowd of 42,793.

Saints were naturally keen to atone for their humiliating defeat at the hands of Leigh on the same pitch 12 months earlier, and the omens looked good when Peter Metcalfe landed a penalty goal after 10 minutes, but Saints were rocked back on their heels when former Knowsley Road favourite Harry Street touched down for Wigan.

And worse was to come for shell-shocked Saints when the Riversiders' scrum-half Johnny Alty linked up with New

49

Zealand winger Brian Nordgren to send Jack Fleming under the posts for Ken Gee to convert, and so increase Wigan's lead to 8-2 with 20 minutes on the clock.

The time was ripe for reading the Riot Act to his team and skipper Duggie duly obliged. Two more penalty goals from Metcalfe's trusty boot meant hitherto-struggling Saints were back into serious contention just before the half-time whistle.

It appeared at this juncture that Wigan had shot their bolt, with Duggie and block-busting second-rowers George Parsons and Bill Bretherton (a Wiganer) setting an inspiring example, and so it proved as a Saints side now with the scent of victory in their nostrils scored two superbly engineered tries, and left Wigan pointless in the second half.

Consequently it came as no surprise when elusive speed merchant Jimmy Honey had the Knowsley Road supporters in raptures with a brilliant solo touchdown goaled by Metcalfe. Then, in the closing moments, Steve Llewellyn unleashed a towering up-and-under which saw Glyn Moses leap like a salmon to steal the ball from Jack Cunliffe and plunge over, with Metcalfe adding his fifth goal.

This late flurry by Saints set the seal on what had ranked among the best Lancashire Cup Finals in the competition's sometimes chequered history, both for sheer drama and grinding intensity along with Saints' refusal to submit in notching 14 unanswered points. The final score was 16-8 to St Helens. The teams were:

St Helens: Glyn Moses; Steve Llewellyn, Duggie Greenall (capt.), Don Gullick, Stan McCormick; Peter Metcalfe, Jimmy Honey; Alan Prescott, Reg Blakemore, George Parr, George Parsons, Bill Bretherton, Vince Karalius.

Wigan: Jack Cunliffe; Brian Nordgren, Jack Broome, Ernie Ashcroft (capt.), Ronnie Hurst; Jack Fleming, Johnny Alty; Ken Gee, Ronnie Mather, Nat Silcock, Bill Collier, Tommy Horrocks, Harry Street.

In the wake of the Championship victory over Halifax just four months earlier Duggie and his team were once again mobbed by Saints' adoring fans as the Lancashire Cup was presented in front of the main stand at Swinton. Incidentally this was the first time that the trophy was bound for St Helens since the 10-2 success against St Helens Recs at Warrington in 1926.

"Like today, winning against Wigan was always something special," said Duggie. "And Saints let their hair down after this one with a wee dram or two of the hard stuff in the dressing room, and I can recall chairman Harry Cook proposing a toast to more success in 1954, in particular another trip to Wembley."

But it was not to be, for although finishing third in the league table with 28 wins in 36 games, Saints' lost 11-0 in the top-four play-off at Warrington. And their Challenge Cup dreams were in for a rude awakening with a 12-5 reverse to Huddersfield at Fartown.

1953-54 had yet again proved another gruelling campaign, with Saints figuring in 45 matches. Llewellyn, Duggie and Metcalfe appeared in more than 40 of these with Llew running in 37 tries, Greenall 17 and rising star Peter Metcalfe 22. Metcalfe also kicked 145 goals.

Duggie commented: "We were all knackered and injuries inevitably took their toll. But winning three trophies in two seasons – including the Lancashire League in 1952-53 – was just reward for Saints' efforts and those of coach Jim Sullivan, who had instilled an unshakeable belief in our ability to pick up silverware."

Duggie's international career developed during this season. He played twice for England in the European Championship. He scored a try against Wales at Knowsley Road in a 24-5 win. Then Swinton winger Peter Norburn scored four tries for England against Other Nationalities at Wigan on 28 November 1953 and Duggie made them all according to press reports. England won 30-22. Duggie also scored for the Whites against the Reds in a 17-17 draw test trial at Headingley on 24 February. A further representative appearance had come earlier in the season, for Lancashire against Cumberland at Whitehaven.

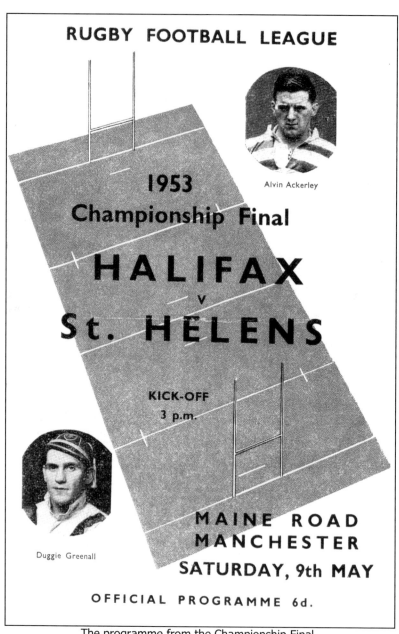

RUGBY FOOTBALL LEAGUE

Alvin Ackerley

1953
Championship Final

HALIFAX
v
St. HELENS

KICK-OFF
3 p.m.

Duggie Greenall

MAINE ROAD
MANCHESTER
SATURDAY, 9th MAY

OFFICIAL PROGRAMME 6d.

The programme from the Championship Final.
(Courtesy RFL)

Duggie Greenall receives the League Championship trophy from Lord Derby at Maine Road, Manchester in 1953.

Captain Duggie Greenall is chaired by his team-mates after the Championship success against Halifax. Other Saints players in the picture are, left to right, John Dickinson, George Parr, Alan Prescott, Reg Blakemore, Bill Bretherton, George Parsons and Don Gullick.

St Helens with the League Championship and Lancashire League trophies in 1953. Back, left to right: Ray Cale, Wilf Roach, George Parsons, Vince Karalius. Middle: Alan Prescott, Steve Llewellyn, Bill Bretherton, Bill Whittaker, Don Gullick, George Parr. Front: Reg Blakemore, Peter Metcalfe, Stan McCormick, Duggie Greenall (captain), Glyn Moses, John Dickinson. Kneeling: George Langfield, Jimmy Honey.

7. A Lions tourist

It is generally accepted in rugby league circles that the greatest honour a player can aspire to is selection for an Australian tour, and with it the coveted accolade of becoming a British Lion.

And, following his exploits against the Kangaroos in Britain in 1952, plus leading Saints to the League Championship in the next year, Duggie Greenall was an automatic choice in the 26-man squad that jetted down under in 1954. The full squad was:

Dickie Williams, Alf Burnell, Geoff Gunney (Hunslet);Ernie Ashcroft, Billy Boston, Jack Cunliffe, Nat Silcock (Wigan); Jim Bowden, Brian Briggs, Dave Valentine (Huddersfield); Frank Castle, Phil Jackson (Barrow); Teddy Cahill (Rochdale Hornets); Duggie Greenall, Alan Prescott (St. Helens); Tommy Harris (Hull); Gerry Helme and Ray Price (Warrington); John Henderson (Workington); Lewis Jones, Andrew Turnbull (Leeds); Tom McKinney (Salford); Terry O'Grady (Oldham); Charlie Pawsey (Leigh); Ken Traill (Bradford Northern); Jack Wilkinson (Halifax).

However, given his alleged tackling transgressions in that explosive home test series – which were blown up by the Australian media - it was inevitable that Duggie's reception would be both hostile and curious as soon as he set foot in Sydney airport. With this in mind, Duggie asked Warrington's Australian forward Harry Bath what were the best places to visit down under and he succinctly replied "hospitals".

Both Saints and Jim Sullivan harboured grave doubts as to whether Duggie should board the plane at Manchester, which would carry the first-ever British rugby league party to fly to Australia.

But the legend lacking nothing in derring-do would have none of this negative advice, although Duggie had a daunting foretaste of what he might expect while enjoying a quiet drink in the Royal Raven Hotel, St Helens.

Mine host at this Church Street watering hole was Saints director Albert Owen, and he quickly referred Duggie to a newspaper article written by former Australian test cricketer Sid Barnes, which suggested that the Kangaroos undertake a course of unarmed combat because it would mean every man for himself once 'the assassin' from St Helens arrived.

Undeterred at this hint of guerrilla warfare to come, Duggie embarked on the four-month trip with relish, but he vehemently denied checking in at Manchester airport with a shopping bag containing just two pairs of underpants and string vests. However, he did concede that it was always his policy to travel light.

Globetrotter Duggie and his team-mates certainly saw something of the world on the outward flight, for the route from England was via Rome, Nice, Karachi, Calcutta, Bangkok, Singapore, Jakarta and Darwin prior to touching down in Sydney.

Predictably, once within the arrivals lounge the entire British squad was besieged by a swarming press corps of reporters and photographers, with Duggie being the main focus of their attention with his no-quarter-asked-or-given reputation having gone before him.

Astounded media men could hardly believe their eyes that such a slightly built, unpretentious figure, could have wreaked such havoc among their fellow countrymen in 1952. Nonetheless, their sporting pages gave him the full treatment, with a typical headline thundering out the momentous message that 'The Bad Man Arrives Today!'

All this was alongside a king-sized picture of Duggie which dominated front pages throughout the rugby league heartlands of New South Wales and Queensland. Meanwhile reporters were frisking Greenall – "they were searching for plaster casts," he quipped - and also implored him to give them Jolsonesque renditions of *Mammy* and *Swanee*.

Reflecting on that never-to-be-forgotten morning at Sydney airport Duggie said: "It was only later that a policeman told me that, as we landed, Frank Sinatra was taking off from the next runway. But no one was interested; they just wanted to see some awesome guy from England called Greenall."

The Great Britain party settled in at the up-market Oceanic Hotel close to Coogee beach, where Duggie found himself rooming with his Saints' buddy Alan Prescott and Charlie Pawsey of Leigh, while Thatto Heath-born Ted Cahill, of Rochdale Hornets, was based in the next room before returning home early due to injury.

On the field Great Britain made an unimpressive start in losing three of their opening six matches, including defeats to a combined Sydney line-up 32-25 and the powerful New South Wales team 22-11, with a later confrontation versus NSW abandoned after 56 minutes because of repeated brawling.

That first game against NSW, the 22-11 defeat, came immediately before the first test at Sydney Cricket Ground, and is one reason why Duggie did not play in any of the three tests in Australia. Both Duggie and his opposite number Harry Wells suffered serious head injuries. They had been gunning for each other throughout, with Wells breaking a cheekbone following a tackle by Duggie, who subsequently had eight stitches inserted into his head resulting from a collision with NSW skipper Clive Churchill.

Duggie was also in the wars after cracking three ribs and these injuries ruled him out of the first test, which Australia won 37-12 at the Sydney Cricket Ground. Great Britain kept faith with the original centre pairing of Phil Jackson and Ernie Ashcroft in winning the second test 38-21 in Brisbane and also in the decider which they lost 20-16 on returning to Sydney.

Said Duggie: "Admittedly I had been warned by our managers Tom Hesketh and Hector Rawson to take things easy and let the Australians, who were coached by Vic Hey, forget what had happened in England in 1952. But there was no question of me being shielded from crowds baying for my blood or certain Kangaroos really after it.

"After all I did turn out in several state fixtures, including torrid encounters in Queensland and Newcastle, and appeared in 21 matches in Australia and New Zealand and scored 13 tries so I reckon I did more than my fair share on that often controversial trip to the other side of the globe.

"As for suggestions of dirty play I totally refuted this charge and regularly stated that my tackling was within the rugby league rules that applied in the mid-1950s. I bore no ill-will to any Australian player, and sincerely believed that professional rugby was my business and intended to keep it that way for as long as possible."

With the benefit of hindsight Duggie was suitably succinct in summing up his love-hate relationship with the Australians:

"I could not understand what all the fuss was about. Yes, I made some enemies, but I also made a lot of friends. I believe that much of the bad feeling towards me down under was stirred up by their trainer 'Coogee' Turner in 1954."

Tour vice-captain Ernie Ashcroft put the 'Greenall man eater' myth into more realistic perspective in an article published in the *Manchester Evening Chronicle* in September 1954. The former Wigan centre and captain commented: "A passage in the Rugby League Council's report of incidents during the tour refers to the mental attitude of a minority of players towards the game itself. You can add to that a section of the Australian press, whom I am convinced were largely responsible for Duggie Greenall's failure to hit top form, of which we all knew he was capable.

"Back home we used to laugh at stories cabled from Australia of how the 1952 tourists to Britain regarded Duggie as a teak-tough, man eating type of centre, with a devastating tackling approach that included an arm encased in plaster. When we arrived in Sydney we discovered it was anything but a joke because the Duggie myth had become reality. Officials, players and fans had swallowed the lot hook, line and sinker. It did not seem to worry Greenall for a week or two, but the Kangaroos appeared to put in that little extra when tackling him.

"It affected his rugby and he became involved in several incidents which, along with criticism by the fans in certain situations, were not calculated to help him reach his best form as an outstanding centre always ready to make openings for his winger. It was all very well for those at home to say he should have ignored those damaging remarks but things don't always work out that way. The difference was particularly noticeable in New Zealand, where Duggie regained something like his best form to earn a place in the second Test."

Now it was time to jet across the Tasman Sea to New Zealand for another three-match test series, the first and last being played at Auckland and the second at Greymouth on South Island. Great Britain won the series 2-1 with 27-7 and 12-6 victories in Auckland, while the Kiwis triumphed 20-14 at Greymouth on a day when Duggie made an impressive comeback to test rugby. The teams were:

Great Britain: Lewis Jones; Billy Boston, Phil Jackson, Duggie Greenall, Terry O'Grady; Dickie Williams, Gerry Helme; Alan Prescott, Tommy Harris, Jack Wilkinson, Brian Briggs, Geoff Gunney, Dave Valentine.

New Zealand: D. White; V. Bakalich, T. O. Baxter, R. Ackland, J. Edwards; W. Sorenson, J. S. Haig; C. R. Johnson, D. L. Blanchard, W. McLennan, J. Butterfield, F. Mulcare, A. Atkinson.

O'Grady and Wilkinson scored tries for the Lions, with Lewis Jones kicking four goals. For New Zealand, Butterfield and Atkinson touched down, with White contributing seven goals.

Skipper Williams and his men also figured in a number of provincial games in New Zealand and Duggie has good reason to relive an eyeball-to-eyeball clash with a representative side at Dunedin on South Island: "I was in hot water again after crash-tackling their stand-off Don White. As he was stretchered off the crowd let me know what they thought of my challenge although I was not penalised. I had to run the gauntlet of the angry mob after the match as we left for the safety of the Great Britain hotel."

Remarkably, given the time, trouble and financial outlay involved, the Great Britain squad then flew back to Australia for an additional four games against, as Duggie puts it, "up-country" opposition. "We were told the return trip was a money-spinner because attendances in Australia had been good so far. From a cash point of view the 26-man party received a weekly allowance as did their wives at home, while the tour bonus was £500, which in the 1950s was quite a considerable sum."

With the rigours of rugby league now on the back-burner Great Britain wound up what had proved a demanding three months with a brief holiday in exotic Hawaii, which included trips to Honolulu and Pearl Harbor. "Visiting the American Naval memorial to the 1,777 personnel who perished when their fleet was bombed by the Japanese in 1941 was quite emotional," reflected a misty-eyed Duggie who, as previously stated, remains very much maritime-oriented.

Then, with a mountain of kit packed, everyone accounted for and passports at the ready, the time to go home had at last arrived, and Duggie's encyclopaedic memory effortlessly recalls the flight-path to England, which this time was via San

Francisco, Boston, Chicago, New York, Newfoundland, Shannon and on to Heathrow.

He says: "My wife Vera and Alan Prescott's better-half Frances were waiting for us on landing, and on passing through customs I remember thinking that I had 'slightly' more luggage than on the outward journey, because I bought all manner of souvenirs for the extended Greenall family after what had been an experience of a lifetime. Then it was a welcome change to board a train to Liverpool after being up in the air so often while on tour."

Duggie's final word on that eventful trek to the Antipodes 52 years ago, is that he is adamant his Saints' team-mates - the spectacular Steve Llewellyn, tackler-supreme Glyn Moses, six-inch nail bender Bill Bretherton and 'Mister Consistency' George Parsons - should have been included. "They all played well in the tour trials at Swinton and Headingley, and if they had been chosen Saints would have had six players in the squad, as they did in 1958."

No story of Duggie Greenall's life is complete without the thoughts of close friend Tommy Bracken, a Saints fanatic whose love of rugby league has taken him from St Helens to Australia: "It was during my short-pants days in 1948 that I became aware of the 'greatest game,' and being born and bred in Thatto Heath and Portico (Donkey Common), I suppose what developed into a lifelong commitment was inevitable. Being a pupil at St. Austin's school helped to boost my unflagging interest, for it was often said that the two 'Rs' of rugby league and religion held sway on the curriculum, which was orchestrated by headmaster Gerry Landers.

"He steered our team to soaring successes in town and county competitions, which was highly commendable when it is remembered that St Austin's was just a small village school, but one blessed with an abundance of oval-ball talent. Over the years these included Rugby League Hall of Fame member Alex Murphy, his half-back partner and World Cup hero Austin Rhodes, tourist Ted Cahill, Peter Metcalfe, Tommy Finn, brothers Frank, Tony and Billy Barrow, Arthur Pimblett and Billy Sheffield. Thatto Heath was, and still is, a fertile breeding ground for future stars.

"From this background, my generation of youngsters was part of the exodus of fans who, on alternate Saturday afternoons, went to Knowsley Road to support the Saints, having first trekked through Taylor Park, and onto Dunriding Lane, before paying a tanner admission to the boys' pen.

"In the late 1940s and right through the 1950s Greenall became inextricably linked to Saints as fish are to chips. In the early days the team was labelled captain Jim Stott and 12 others, while the pack was dubbed 'the easy six' a name derived from a well-known football coupon. It was then that the gifted Greenall first emerged as a versatile utility player, prior to settling into his accustomed role as right centre to Welshman Steve Llewellyn.

"Time marched on without silverware for Saints, but all that changed with the arrival of master coach Jim Sullivan in 1952, and skipper Duggie enjoyed a leading role in subsequent team triumphs, which included the Championship and Challenge Cup victories.

"The 1954 British Lions squad in Australia included Duggie, and by now his reputation had reached the faraway shores of Australia. The Australians thought Duggie stood six feet six inches, tipped the scales at 17 stone, and girded himself with a plaster cast on that famous right arm.

"His media reception at Sydney airport was massive, such was the cult figure aura surrounding a player constantly under the spotlight and in the wars due to his uncompromising approach to the demands of rugby league.

"My friend the late Ted Cahill often told me tales of the escapades involving Duggie and himself. 'We would swap positions just before the final whistle so that Greenall could make a dash to the tunnel before the crowd could get him after he had given Mammy to the odd Aussie or two.' I can well recall Cahill telling me that in one match he shouted to Duggie 'Are you trying to get us all killed?' after he had caused mayhem with his merciless tackling. Twenty years later I was escorting an Australian businessman around where I worked and he inquired if I was a Saints supporter. When I enlightened him he exploded 'is that f-------g Duggie Greenall still around?' He then astounded me by re-living all the hype from 1954. He then informed me that he was a director and later chairman of the Manly club and we remain friends to this day. For somewhat different reasons Douglas Greenall had crossed our respective paths."

The Great Britain team for Duggie's test debut in 1951. Back, left to right:
Bob Ryan (Warrington), Ernest Ward (Bradford) captain, Ken Gee (Wigan),
Duggie Greenall (St Helens), Cec Thompson (Hunslet), Vince McKeating
(Workington), Billy Blan (Wigan), Elwyn Gwyther (Belle Vue Rangers).
Front: Dick Cracknell (Huddersfield), Alf Burnell (Hunslet), Dickie Williams
(Leeds), Jack Cunliffe (Wigan), George Wilson (Workington).
(Photo: Courtesy Robert Gate)

Ray Price, Duggie Greenall and Dickie Williams sporting their Great Britain
shirts at the RFL's headquarters in Leeds, in 1951.

The Great Britain side that lost 27-7 against Australia at Odsal in 1952.
Back, left to right: Charlie Pawsey (Leigh), Alan Prescott (St Helens),
Jim Featherstone (Warrington), Tom McKinney (Salford), Ernest Ward
(Bradford, captain), Dave Valentine (Huddersfield), Dai Bevan (Wigan),
Ken Traill (Bradford). Front: Duggie Greenall (St Helens),
Willie Horne (Barrow), Ted Toohey (Barrow),
Frank Castle (Barrow), Jack Evans (Hunslet).

The 1954 Great Britain Lions squad that toured Australia and New Zealand.
Back: E. Cahill, A. Turnbull, W. J. Boston, J. Wilkinson,
J. B. Henderson, J. Cunliffe, T. McKinney Standing: T. P. O'Grady,
J. Bowden, K. Traill, N. D. Silcock, C. H. Pawsey, G. Gunney,
B. Briggs, G. A Prescott. Seated: D. Greenall, B. L. Jones,
E. J. Ashcroft, H. Rawson, R. L. Williams, T. Hesketh, P. B. Jackson,
D. D. Valentine, F. Castle. Front: A. Burnell, P. T. Harris,
H. R. Price, G. J. Helme. (Both photos courtesy Robert Gate)

All dressed up – and somewhere to go! St Helens giants of the past at the Rugby League centenary celebrations in Huddersfield in 1995. Back, left to right: John Mantle, Mick Murphy, Alex Murphy, Ray French, Peter Harvey, George Nicholls, Kel Coslett. Front Geoff Pimblett, Austin Rhodes, Glyn Moses, Alan Prescott, Bob Dagnall, Duggie Greenall.

Hundred up! Duggie Greenall, Tom van Vollenhoven and Brian Glover at St Helens centenary celebrations at Knowsley Road in 1990. (Photo: Alex Service)

8. Trouble at t' mill

So, glad to be home following a somewhat chequered time down under, Duggie enjoyed a short break reliving his tour experiences to his countless adoring fans in St Helens and further afield.

But now it was time to get back to the nitty-gritty of work-a-day living, but when globetrotting Duggie returned to the Triplex factory at Eccleston expecting a hero's welcome, he was due for a rude awakening from his foreman Arthur Spottiswood.

Desperately disappointed Duggie was told that he could not restart work in the fitting shop until he had paid his subscription arrears to the Amalgamated Engineering Union otherwise his workmates would embark on strike action.

A chastened Duggie recalled: "I did not realise that I had to pay union dues while on tour, and immediately coughed up the three-month backlog of cash. To be honest I think some of my colleagues resented me being absent for so long, and also having two jobs by playing for Saints on Saturday afternoons.

"I brought them duty-free cigarettes and souvenirs as goodwill gestures and certainly not as peace offerings, because the management and staff had given me a rousing send-off when I had left for Australia. The whole business left a nasty taste in my mouth, so I decided there and then that the time had come to leave Triplex, where I had been employed since 1941. I was then 27 years old, married with a young son and a mortgage, so it was obvious that I needed another job. However they did give me a farewell do in the canteen when gaffer Arthur Spottiswood wished me all the best, told me I could keep my tool kit comprising a 7/16ths spanner and left-handed screwdriver, but warned me that I could not take the lathe that I had been leaning on for the past 13 years.

"After talking the matter over with my wife Vera we made the decision to look for a public house, which would be my first taste of life behind the pumps, but obviously not what flowed from them.

Saints' director Arthur Naylor, who was an executive at the local brewery Greenalls (that name is purely coincidental) arranged for me to take over the licence of the Victoria Tap in St Helens Market, just a drop-kick away from the by-now demolished Churn Inn.

"It was a typical old-fashioned ale-house, complete with bar and spittoons, snug and singing room equipped with a honky-tonk piano where, as a break from pulling pints and serving pie-and-peas, I grabbed the microphone and wowed the regulars with *Mammy* and *Swanee*.

"Word got around that I was at the 'Vic' and the Saints fan base who gathered there was boosted by market traders and shoppers dropping in at lunchtime for the occasional gill or a more relaxed slurping session after work.

"I soon realised that I had found my true vocation on the business side of the bar, and the Victoria Tap proved to be the forerunner to three other watering holes where I was landlord, aided and abetted, of course, by Vera.

Membership of the Greenall Whitley golfing society and the Licensed Victuallers' Association followed, and all this broadened our horizons with holidays both here in England and overseas. We made many lasting friendships as a result. My, was I going up in the world, but I managed to keep my feet firmly on the ground."

Season 1954-55 dawned and, as is often the case after a period of soaring success, the new campaign was to be one of transition both in terms of results and personnel. Saints went out of the Lancashire Cup 20-8 at Oldham, the Challenge Cup 14-4 at Workington, and finished seventh in the League table with 25 wins in 36 games.

Outspoken Duggie found himself in a spot of bother with the referee following that highly-charged third-round clash on Cumbrian soil on a freezing March afternoon. For, as the teams were leaving the pitch, Duggie was allegedly heard to doubt the official's parentage after he had allowed a crucial try to Workington.

The upshot was that Saints secretary Bert Murray received notification from the Rugby Football League disciplinary committee that the controversial centre had been suspended for two matches. The annoyed Duggie remained adamant that the charge was nothing but hearsay and the ban was lifted on appeal.

Players come and players go and that was the pattern at Saints in 1954-55 with seven of the Wembley squad that faced Huddersfield in 1953 seeking pastures new. They were Don Gullick, Stan McCormick, Jimmy Honey, George Langfield, George Parr, Reg Blakemore and Ray Cale.

In addition to them, long-serving Joe Ball was en-route for Barrow and Widnesian Bill Whittaker for Liverpool City, while Peter Metcalfe was compelled to retire through injury. Taking due account of all this it will be understood that a gale-force wind of change was blowing through Knowsley Road.

Rock-like Duggie stood firm, however, to witness the advance of a certain Vincent Peter Patrick Karalius, the signing of Nat Silcock from Wigan, the return of Bill Finnan from Salford and - at the same time - a clutch of talented youngsters coming through from St Helens schools and amateur league rugby.

They included Frank Carlton, Alec Davies, Eric Ledger, Walter Delves, Roy Robinson, Josh Gaskell, brothers Albert 'Ab' and Fred Terry, plus the dynamic half-back duo from St Austin's school: Austin Rhodes and Alex Murphy.

Dubbed the 'Wild Bull of the Pampas' by the Australian media, Vince Karalius is now 73 and lives on the Isle of Man. He has many memories of Duggie: "My first team debut was against Warrington at Wilderspool in 1952. The Wire had a side bristling with talent including Brian Bevan, Gerry Helme, Ray Price, Ally Naughton, Harold Palin and big Australian forward Harry Bath.

"The ground was packed with many spectators sitting on touchline seats. I had never experienced anything like it and the atmosphere was electric. I ran out last as I always did and began to warm up for the battle to come.

"Just then Duggie sauntered to the centre spot, cupped his hands and shouted 'Bathy, which war did you fight in? You are not far from Japan. We should have bombed you bastards along with the Japanese.' I could not believe it. I thought he would start a war, and he did.

"No matter who Saints played he usually told his opposite number 'I'm going to break your jaw' and, take it from me, Duggie smashed quite a few. I called him the hired assassin.

When I was on tour in 1958 I asked Oldham's Alan Davies how he coped with Duggie and he replied: 'Every time I faced him I told him that I was going to have him that afternoon. Then I woke up.'

"However there was another side to Duggie, because he had a great sense of humour. I remember being selected with him for a representative game against the touring Kiwis and, with it being my first honour, I was naturally very excited.

"The fixture was at Odsal Stadium, Bradford. In those days Duggie ran a pub called The Engine in Parr and he told me to call for him so that we could travel to Yorkshire together.

"His wife Vera let me in and told me to sit in the lounge of their living quarters. It was the first time that I had been in the place and I sat on the edge of chair just looking around.

"All of a sudden a big rabbit came bounding across the room from behind the television. Duggie came in with half a Guinness in his hand, laughing his head off. He did not say a word about the rabbit, finished his drink, put a jacket on, and we set off for Shaw Street railway station.

"On the way to the train we both bought something to read for the 60-mile journey. I purchased the *Daily Herald* and *Daily Dispatch* newspapers, while Duggie settled for *The Dandy* and *The Beano* comics. Say no more.

"Duggie turned out at 11 stone and a bit or thereabouts. I am sure his heart accounted for most of that. His defence was magnificent, he was a superb tactician and playmaker and I loved being in the same side as him.

"Would he fit into today's game? Yes. Just imagine: full-time professionalism, modern training techniques and dietary regimes. Duggie would probably have been a couple of stone heavier and five yards faster. He would be both lethal and sensational.

"How do I rate him? In my book *Lucky Thirteen* he was included in my world team. I think that says it all. Duggie is also still my pal."

The arrival of the resourceful Austin Rhodes at Saints sparked a memory-jerking reunion with Greenall, for the perennial pair had first met at Triplex, behind the Eccleston

End at Knowsley Road in 1952, when Austin began work as an apprentice tool-maker.

"I had heard he was a promising utility player," said Duggie in a masterpiece of understatement. "From the moment Austin made his debut towards the end of the season I could see he had it in him to make the grade in the professional game, while his goalkicking was a big bonus."

Austin Rhodes was also complimentary in his tribute to one of the glass town's most celebrated sporting sons in saying: "When I was first introduced to Duggie he was already well established at Saints, but at work he was equally famous for an uncanny ability to spear metal washers with files minus handles from distances of around six feet. He was also adept at operating a metal-cutting machine so accurately that the tradesman rarely needed to use a file afterwards. Apart from these great talents his boss Arthur Spottiswood was quite content to listen to Duggie singing *Mammy* the length and breadth of the fitting shop.

"The caring Duggie immediately took me under his wing when I signed for Saints aged 16 in 1953. He was the original rough diamond, and the story goes that on leaving Manchester airport for Australia and New Zealand he turned up in just the clothes he stood up in, plus a change of Marks and Spencer's underwear and 10 bob in his pocket.

"One of my first games for Saints was against Belle Vue Rangers and I was dealt a smack in the mouth and lost a couple of teeth. Duggie then had a long chat with me at Triplex on the following Monday and taught me how to look after myself at lot better.

"I recall hard-man Duggie broke his jaw against Leeds in the opening five minutes but stayed on the field throughout the 80 minutes without batting an eyelid, and it was only after the match that he was persuaded to go to hospital to have the fractured jaw re-set and wired up.

"On the field his timing of the tackle was split-second and he stopped many a try when the opposition had an overlap by crash-tackling the inside centre, stand-off or wide-running second-rower.

"He believed that Nat Silcock was the best-ever attacking forward, but his real hero was Vince Karalius, whom he would have backed against American world heavyweight boxing champion Rocky Marciano in the 1950s.

"Without doubt Duggie ranks among the most unforgettable characters to figure in rugby league both at test and club level, and I regarded it as a privilege to have shared dressing room pegs with him at Knowsley Road. Long away journeys seemed much shorter on hearing his renderings of musical hits of the day fortified, of course, on homeward-bound treks with the odd livener. He also loved to tell hilarious tales of his stint in the Air Training Corps during the war."

However, the biggest sensation involving Duggie at Saints exploded in January 1955 when, along with Peter Metcalfe and Bill Bretherton, he submitted a transfer request, all three of which were refused point-blank. Referring to skipper Duggie's bombshell, chairman Harry Cook said: "My board do not want him to leave Knowsley Road but we do feel that Duggie needs a rest after 10 seasons of continuous rugby, which has left him under the weather."

In recent weeks, particularly against Wakefield Trinity on the previous Saturday at Knowsley Road, Duggie had been upset by the crowd's attitude towards him. He had been below his best for most of the season and once-loyal supporters had let Duggie know it. He had suggested to Saints that a change of club might be better for all concerned. Duggie had also been annoyed by adverse remarks before the Australian tour, and the barracking from the Knowsley Road terraces had inflamed the situation.

Reflecting on the supporters' reaction half a century later, Duggie said: "Constructive criticism was one thing but it was below the belt to have to listen to scathing comments such as 'get off the field Greenall, you're just like your ale - p--- poor'. Enough was enough."

Saints rested Duggie for the next fixture against Blackpool Borough at home, but the resilient, if aggrieved, icon bounced back to play in 14 games before the end of what had been an unsettling season. All this was further compounded when Duggie was relieved of the team captaincy in favour of Alan Prescott.

9. Challenge Cup glory at last

Season 1955-56 held little promise of an upsurge in fortunes for Saints after the previous barren campaign, but they were not to know that rugby league's most prestigious prize lay on the distant horizon.

The Challenge Cup was proudly placed on the Knowsley Road sideboard for the first time since the competition's inception in 1897, when Saints lost 10-3 to Batley. Three subsequent final defeats followed by Huddersfield 37-3 in 1915, Widnes 10-3 in 1930, and Huddersfield again, 15-10 in 1953.

An indifferent season prior to the Cup run included a shock 18-12 defeat at Barrow in the opening round of the Lancashire Cup. The lack of a goalkicker cost Saints dearly for they scored four tries through Duggie, Nat Silcock, Brian Howard and Frank Carlton, with no conversion in sight.

"It was just one of those days," sighed a rueful Duggie. "Austin Rhodes – who finished the season with 140 goals – hadn't yet taken over the kicking role and Billy Blan, Bill Finnan and myself were all off target, otherwise Saints would probably have made it into the second round."

One highlight away from Knowsley Road came on 7 December. Duggie played centre for a Northern Rugby League XIII against the New Zealand tourists at Odsal. His team beat the Kiwis 24-11. Duggie scored a try, and it was the only time he played at centre with all-time leading try-scorer Brian Bevan as his winger.

This season the league table was decided on a percentage basis because of the late withdrawal of Belle Vue Rangers leaving a gap in the fixtures. Saints finished third with 27 victories in 34 games, while some clubs played the full complement of 36 matches. Unfortunately, the top-four play-off saw Saints lose 23-8 at Halifax's Thrum Hall, on a day when John Dickinson suffered a knee injury which caused him to miss the Wembley Final.

Saints' sometimes rocky road to the Twin Towers began with a 15-6 home win against Warrington, and this was followed by a 48-5 thrashing of Castleford with Steve Llewellyn scoring six tries, again at Knowsley Road. A trio of home ties was completed with the visit of Bradford Northern, whom Saints put to the sword to the tune of 53-6 on an afternoon when hooker Frank McCabe broke his ankle and had to hang up his boots.

"Here again it was sheer bad luck for 'Darkie', as we called Frank," said Duggie. "He had made the number nine jersey his own in 1955-56, and the fracture happened in an innocuous tackle when he scored his second try. McCabe's hopes of a Wembley appearance had been dashed."

By now soaring Saints' dreams of the ultimate Challenge Cup showdown in London were on a high, but they first had to surmount the daunting obstacle set by holders Barrow in the semi-final at Station Road, Swinton, before the burning ambition of Saints skipper Alan Prescott's side might be realised.

A nail-biting 5-5 draw followed, with Carlton scoring Saints' try which was converted by Rhodes before a massive 38,897 attendance. Extra time was not played so the scene was set for a replay at Wigan's Central Park on the following Wednesday with a 5.00pm kick-off, because Central Park had no floodlights in those days.

Such was the interest generated by this encore blockbuster by Saints and the Shipbuilders that numerous special trains, plus hundreds of coaches and cars converged on Wigan from St Helens and Barrow, posing huge traffic problems for the police. Looking back on that afternoon of grinding gridlock in town-centre Wallgate Duggie said: "Saints' coach had to be escorted by police motorcycle outriders in order to reach Central Park in time for the kick-off, and many fans only got into the ground after the game had started."

The attendance was 44,731 and what was set before them, while not a feast of rugby league football, was nonetheless a typical cup-tie of no-quarter-asked-or-given intensity which remained scoreless after 80 minutes, with the ultimate decision of who should face Halifax at Wembley settled only after extra time.

What had resolved itself into a forward-oriented battle royal raged on almost interminably, with both Saints and Barrow striving to break the deadlock. No prisoners were taken with Vince Karalius for Saints and St Helens-born Jack

Grundy of Barrow particularly in the wars. Karalius, in fact, had part of an ear torn off. "Don't worry, just stick it back on," exclaimed the teak-tough Widnesian.

When the stalemate at the end of normal time was signalled by referee Matt Coates, the packed Central Park crowd rose in salute to the efforts of Saints and Barrow, but it was increasingly obvious that something extraordinary was needed to set the scoreboard ticking at long last.

Cometh the hour cometh the man. Let Duggie take up a story of *Boy's Own* dimensions: "There were just seconds left of the first 10 minutes of extra time and Barrow were camped near Saints' try-line. On running the ball out our full-back Glyn Moses fed Llewellyn with the opposition line 80 yards away, and Llew handed off Frank Castle and John 'Dinks' Harris, rounded Ted Toohey and beat Castle again before diving over."

Rhodes converted after the pitch had been cleared of ecstatic Saints' supporters, and although Barrow captain Willie Horne's penalty goal made the score 5-2 there was a gut feeling abroad that Prescott's men were nearly at Wembley. Saints' second try by George Parsons was again goaled by Rhodes and this confirmed that belief, while Grundy's touchdown for Barrow in the dying moments was of no more than consolation value.

However the night belonged to Abertillery-born schoolmaster Steve Llewellyn. Reflecting on his epic semi-final try he was modesty-personified as he remembered: "I only realised how important it was when I went into the Grange Park Hotel after the match and everyone wanted to buy me a drink."

St Helens: Glyn Moses; Steve Llewellyn, Duggie Greenall, Bill Finnan, Frank Carlton; John Dickinson, Austin Rhodes; Alan Prescott (capt.), Len McIntyre, Albert Terry, Nat Silcock, George Parsons, Vince Karalius.

Barrow: Ted Toohey; Jim Lewthwaite, Danny Leatherbarrow, Dennis Goodwin, Frank Castle; Willie Horne (capt.), John Harris; George Woosey, Vince McKeating, Frank Barton, Jack Grundy, Reg Parker, Bill Healy.

Asked for his views on reaching Wembley for the second time in three seasons, Duggie waxed lyrical over that fabulous try from Llewellyn: "It was the best of the 240 he scored for Saints and I should know, because I played centre to Steve more than any other player." Duggie played with Steve Llewellyn in 151 of Steve's 287 games for Saints.

Added the garrulous Duggie: "I was upset when relieved of the Saints captaincy during the close season, but I was right behind Alan Prescott in Saints' bid to bring the Challenge Cup to St Helens for the first time, after experiencing the disappointment of 1953."

A major factor in Saints' success was the try scoring of wingers Frank Carlton with 39 and Steve Llewellyn with 38, who ran riot during the 1955-56 campaign.

Just before Wembley, Saints overcame Whitehaven 22-7 at Knowsley Road on Easter Monday. Predictably, a virtual 'A' team was selected. Even Duggie was left out, with only Parsons of what Saints believed would be the Cup Final XIII included.

But the biggest crowd-puller of all that day was the debut of a scrum-half named Alexander James Murphy, who was hailed as a boy wonder under the tutelage of headmaster Gerry Landers at St Austin's school, within the oval-ball hotbed of Thatto Heath. It is almost superfluous to state how well Murph eventually realised his vast potential on the way to iconic status.

For the record the Saints' 'first' team versus Whitehaven was: Arthur Pimblett; Eric Ledger, Brian Howard, Reg Senior, Alec Davies; Wilf Smith, Alex Murphy; Bill Shiels, Wilf O'Mara, Josh Gaskell, George Parsons, Roy Robinson, Max Garbler. Pimblett scored five goals and Davies three tries.

At this point it is timely to add the thoughts of Alex Murphy on Duggie: "I first met Duggie when I signed for Saints in 1955, but having seen him in action I knew what he was capable of, and sampled this at first hand when I played in the same side as him against Workington at Knowsley Road in 1956.

"Realising that I was just a kid of 17 playing in only his second game in Saints' senior team, Duggie was quick to offer me a friendly word of encouragement, which meant a lot to me coming from a rugby league icon. In those days the game was 80 minutes of sheer physical contact and, with no substitutes allowed, there was no time for a breather and injured players often stayed on the pitch in order to keep 13 men on the field.

"In this respect Duggie's pain threshold bordered on the incredible, and although he was not a big 'un he was totally fearless in facing opponents who were. The timing of his tackling was perfect as was his uncanny ability to draw the defence before putting his wingman away, as Steve Llewellyn and Tom van Vollenhoven soon discovered.

"Duggie was the ideal centre to nurse those two into the rigours of rugby league after leaving the XV-a-side version, particularly when it is remembered that in the 1950s union wingers saw little of the ball nor did much defensive work.

"Gutsy Duggie was a man to have alongside you in the trenches when the battle was at its fiercest, plus being an inspiring leader who could 'read' a game and, as a deep thinker, he lifted the spirits of those around him both in the dressing room and on the field. To coin a phrase, Duggie was like a Wild West gunslinger who was quick on the draw, because he believed that rugby league was all about winning and for that reason he would have been in my side every time.

"My abiding memory of the legend that was Douglas Greenall? That's a hard question to answer but having given the matter a lot of thought. I will go for Saints' 44-22 Championship Final victory against Hunslet at Odsal in 1959. For on that day Duggie had a major role in van Vollenhoven's hat-trick after we looked out for the count when we were trailing 12-4 with just 10 minutes gone.

"Duggie was a born prankster along with being a crooner on the bus which made long journeys to Workington and Hull seem much shorter - what more can one say about the local lad from Dunriding Lane? Not much except to add that, given today's full-time professionalism, Duggie would have been an even greater sensation than he was 50 years ago."

The Wembley build-up was gathering momentum long before the big day approached with Saints' stars once again enjoying celebrity rating, which no doubt influenced the club directors to take them away from it all to a secret hideaway which, according to Duggie, proved to be no further than King George School playing fields, Southport.

St Helens itself was yet again agog with Wembley fever and was bedecked with red and white bunting and similar favours. Shaw Street railway station and the coach firms were inundated with bookings for this eagerly-awaited clash of the Titans on Saturday 28 April, while Duggie's Family Ale at 1/- (5p) a pint and Oatmeal Stout at 1/6d (7p) a pint were flowing in greater profusion than ever at the Victoria Tap.

But only for the thirsty bar flies, because genial mine host Duggie had his mind on other matters - the Challenge Cup Final. He and Saints' squad were totally committed to bringing smiles to the faces of their fanatical supporters.

On a team selection note, and as previously hinted, changes had to be made to Saints' line-up when Todder Dickinson cried off with a recurring knee injury sustained, ironically, at Halifax the week before the Final. Then Walter 'Digger' Delves broke down in training. All this meant that Brian Howard (father of 1990s international player Harvey) came in at centre for Bill Finnan, who switched to stand-off for Dickinson, while forward Roy Robinson, who had been signed from amateur side UGB (United Glass Bottle Manufacturers), deputised for Delves.

Making his Challenge Cup debut in the Final might have proved a nerve-wracking ordeal for Roy, but his reception from Saints' fans on hearing his name on the tannoy worked wonders for his peace of mind. "You could have knocked me down with a feather when coach Jim Sullivan told me at Brighton on Friday that I was an 11th-hour call-up. Go out there and tackle and run yourself to a standstill was his final order," Robinson remembered.

And where was Duggie amid all this chopping and changing? "Keeping a watching brief and not in the slightest concerned," he said, "because I had every confidence in the lads drafted into Saints' side. Howard and Robinson were no strangers to top-flight rugby league."

Formidable Halifax, who finished marginally behind league champions Warrington, were making their fifth appearance beneath the Twin Towers and were widely regarded as the most feared team in Yorkshire. In particular, their dreadnought pack boasted the likes of Jack Wilkinson and captain Alvin Ackerley, while the complete Halifax squad bristled with internationals.

Perhaps the key to Saints' ultimate triumph was the age factor, because streetwise coach Sullivan was adamant in his belief that a Saints team averaging 24 years a man compared to the opposition's 28 would hold the second-half aces of speed and stamina so vital on Wembley's wide open spaces.

"And so it proved," recalled Duggie, "because once Prescott and company had stood toe-to-toe with Wilkinson's 'terrible six' in the first half we knew it was only a matter of time before Halifax cracked. Sullivan's immortal instruction as Saints' took the field for the final 40 minutes was 'sling the ball about and you'll run them off their feet'." Prophetic words indeed.

Upwards of 20,000 Sintelliners were among the 79,341 crowd on a day favoured by brilliant sunshine and wafting breeze for a Challenge Cup Final at which the chief guest was Field Marshal Alexander of Tunis, and the referee was the vastly experienced Ron Gelder of Wakefield.

The opening 40 minutes largely resolved itself into a battle of attrition with Howard and Llewellyn going nearest to scoring for Saints, and Ken Dean and Johnny Freeman doing likewise for Halifax. Rhodes missed with a brace of penalty attempts for the Lancastrians and Tyssul Griffiths was similarly off-target for the men from Thrum Hall and, as against Barrow in the semi-final, the question on every spectator's lips was "Which team is going to break the stranglehold on scoring?"

In stepped the powerful Prescott - enjoying a real captain's knock - to raise the siege with a surging 50-yard break which was at once a great psychological boost and also almost resulted in a try for Carlton. However a marker had been laid towards Saints' left flank and, as the team began to open play out, the touchdown that all St Helens had been praying for was duly delivered - albeit in the 66th minute.

The crucial score was engineered by Moses, Prescott and Karalius, who put Howard away and he eluded Geoff Palmer and Arthur Daniels before timing his pass superbly to the supporting Carlton. Blackbrook boy Carlton swerved past Griffiths on half-way and outpaced Freeman to touch down between the posts. The Saints fans' roar was heard on the radio at Frank's home in O'Sullivan Crescent, where his mother Annie famously remarked "It was a good job my lad didn't knock on."

Rhodes tacked on the goal and, refusing to sit on their lead, Saints consolidated their five-point advantage when Silcock broke through to feed Duggie, and his uncannily timed pass sent Llewellyn over in the corner to become the first Saints' player to score tries in two Wembley finals.

Now more familiar with the capricious Wembley wind currents, Rhodes converted magnificently from the touchline and, although Griffiths' penalty spared Halifax the indignity of a nil return on the scoreboard, Saints had both hands on the silverware when Karalius put Lance Todd Trophy winner Prescott in for the clinching three-pointer for a 13-2 win.

St Helens: Glyn Moses; Steve Llewellyn, Duggie Greenall, Brian Howard, Frank Carlton; Bill Finnan, Austin Rhodes; Alan Prescott (captain), Len McIntyre, Nat Silcock, Roy Robinson, George Parsons, Vince Karalius.

Halifax: Tyssul Griffiths; Arthur Daniels, Tom Lynch, Geoff Palmer, Johnny Freeman; Ken Dean, Stan Kielty; Jack Wilkinson, Alvin Ackerley (captain), John Henderson, Albert Fearnley, Les Pearce, Ken Traill.

Reflecting on the Wembley triumph Duggie said: "Dad came into the Saints' dressing room to see my medal and I told him to put it back into my pocket. But it was panic stations when I put my coat on because the medal was missing. Imagine my relief when George Parsons found the gong in his jacket - I had a strong word or two with Dad later. When we left Wembley my wife Vera - who was dressed in blue and white - boarded the Halifax coach by mistake. You can only guess the good-natured banter that sparked off among the losers' wives."

Then, with presentations and other formalities over, it was back to the Metropole Hotel in Brighton for a celebration banquet and a ditty or two from Duggie in a Mardi Gras-like atmosphere. Sunday was a day of rest and reflection after the exertions and excitement of the previous 24 hours, before what Duggie described as the "icing on the cake" when conquering heroes Saints headed back north, this time with the Challenge Cup for the first time.

That, of course, was the triumphant return to St Helens Town Hall, but before all the revelry there was a word of thanks from Saints' chairman Harry Cook who commented: "The best supporters in the Rugby League have at last had their reward. There were 15,000 of them in Victoria Square in 1953. I'll wager that figure is doubled on Monday."

How right the revered 'Cookie' was for every available police officer was on duty to cope with a 30,000-strong throng, of which more than 300 needed attention from St John's Ambulance attendants. Bedlam reigned when Alan Prescott, Mayor Jane Donald and Saints' officials appeared on the Town Hall steps. Chief Constable Symmonds' appeal for silence was ignored because Saints' euphoric supporters were hell-bent on saluting their team.

"We want Preccy, we want Carlo, we want Llew, we want Todder, we want Duggie," - the chanting went on into the still of the night.

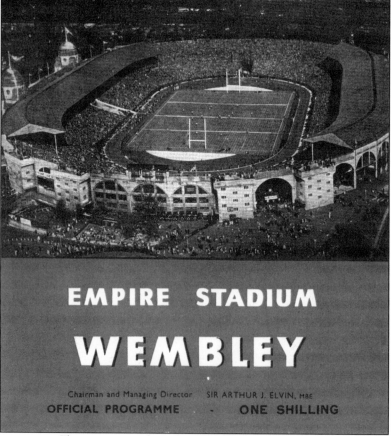

The programme from the 1956 Challenge Cup Final.
(Courtesy RFL)

Wembley in their sights. The Saints' XIII that overcame Barrow 10-5 in the 1956 Challenge Cup semi-final replay at Wigan. Back, left to right: Steve Llewellyn, George Parsons, Ab Terry, Nat Silcock, Glyn Moses, Vince Karalius, Duggie Greenall. Front: Len McIntyre, Alan Prescott (captain), John Dickinson, Bill Finnan, Austin Rhodes, Frank Carlton.

Chairman Harry Cook and captain Alan Prescott lead out St Helens at Wembley. Other players on view are Glyn Moses, Steve Llewellyn, Duggie Greenall, Brian Howard, Frank Carlton, Bill Finnan, Austin Rhodes and Len McIntyre.

St Helens centre Brian Howard is presented to chief guest Earl Alexander of Tunis. Other St Helens players in camera range were, left to right: Bill Finnan, Frank Carlton, Duggie Greenall and Steve Llewellyn.

Bottoms up! Captain Alan Prescott leads the victory toast in the St Helens dressing room following the 13-2 win against Halifax.

Chairman Harry Cook and coach Jim Sullivan admire the Challenge Cup.

At last! The St Helens team with the Challenge Cup. Back, left to right, Duggie Greenall, Roy Robinson, Nat Silcock, Steve Llewellyn, Vince Karalius, George Parsons, Ab Terry, Reg Senior. Front: Len McIntyre, Bill Finnan, Austin Rhodes, Alan Prescott (captain), Jim Sullivan (coach), Glyn Moses, Frank Carlton, John Dickinson, Brian Howard.

St Helens skipper Alan Prescott and his team and their supporters with the Challenge Cup at the Metropole Hotel, Brighton, in 1956.

10. The cupboard was bare

Season 1956-57 was notable for the wrong reasons in that Saints failed to lift a trophy for the first time in the coaching reign of Jim Sullivan - but they went desperately close in two major competitions. Oldham triumphed 10-3 over Alan Prescott's side in the Lancashire Cup Final at Wigan, when the Roughyeds' crucial late try was hotly disputed by Saints. Frank Carlton scored Saints' touchdown in a torrid encounter watched by a crowd of 39,544. The teams were:

Oldham: W. B. Ganley; R. Cracknell, D. M. Ayres, A. Davies, J. Etty; F. Stirrup, F. Pitchford; K. Jackson, J. Keith, D. G. Vines, S. D. Little, C. H. Winslade, D. Turner.

St Helens: G. Moses; S. M. Llewellyn, D. Greenall, W. Finnan, F. Carlton; A. J. Rhodes, J. Dickinson; A. Prescott, L. McIntyre, D. Silcock, G. Parsons, J. Gaskell, V. Karalius.

Holders Saints then went out of the Challenge Cup in the first round by a cliff-hanging 9-8 at Whitehaven with hooker Tom McKinney being sent off for retaliation. Glyn Moses notched both Saints' tries but Jim McMenemy's three-pointer and John McKeown's three goals spelled victory for the Cumbrians.

"No one could blame me for Saints' defeat," remembered Duggie. "I thought I had a good game at Rochdale the previous week, so I was dumbfounded when Sully told me he was 'resting' me in the aftermath." Injuries, however, in particular to the shoulder, had taken their toll on Duggie for he played in only 18 games in that season.

Undoubtedly the highlight of a campaign when the silverware cupboard remained bare was the record 44-2 thrashing of mighty Australia in November. As well as the huge margin of victory the game was also noteworthy in that all six Saints forwards scored a try. Carve their names with pride: skipper Alan Prescott, Frank McCabe, Ab Terry, Nat Silcock, Josh Gaskell and Vince Karalius.

Saints finished fifth in the league table with 25 wins in 38 outings, despite topping the for-and-against points-scoring chart with figures of 902-355, while other items of interest in 1956-57 were that Steve Llewellyn followed up his six tries against Castleford in March with another half-dozen versus Liverpool City at Knotty Ash in August.

"And he might have set another record because Steve had three disallowed, and I sent him over for the majority of them," recollected Duggie. He also recalled the four 'Macs' who wore the number nine shirt for Saints in this period: Tom McKinney, Frank McCabe, John McGuinness and Len McIntyre - each of whom followed in the illustrious steps of the renowned Reg Blakemore.

He also remembers Ruskin Park rugby union winger Sammy Clemson, who appeared in two first team matches for Saints but did not take the professional ticket.

Away from the trials, tribulations and triumphs of rugby league football another transfer was looming for Duggie in 1956, this time concerning his licensed premises. For, having first been called to the bar at the Victoria Tap, he now accepted the daunting challenge of becoming mine host of the Engine Inn, Newton Road, a heavily patronised hostelry nestling in the predominantly working class area of Derbyshire Hill.

Duggie and Vera were an immediate hit with the regulars, and the personable pair quickly ensured that sporting attractions such as darts, dominoes and pool facilities were readily available, along with the inevitable singing room and, as an urgent priority, the dispensing of good ale.

Ever mindful of the need for occasional respite from public house life, Duggie diversified by learning the rudiments of pig breeding and, on converting his garage into a sty and inviting offers of suitable swill, he then brought home the bacon as the piglets were delivered with multi-litter speed.

Not short on business acumen, Duggie then entered into a trading agreement to sell his novel source of income to a St Helens pork butcher - only to discover he was getting a raw deal. "Imagine how I felt when I looked into his window and saw the price was 6 shillings [30p] per pound and I was being paid just 1 shilling [5p]" protested Duggie.

That ill-fated venture petered out and, having dismantled the makeshift piggery, Duggie then joined forces with his Saints team-mates Ab Terry and Nat Silcock as, armed with a 12-bore shotgun, licensed of course, they went in search of 'big' game.

Rabbits and vermin were their immediate quarry found on land behind the Engine Inn before, flushed by their early successes, the intrepid trio trespassed further afield onto the estate of a peer of the realm, and were soon bagging partridge and pheasant, plus the odd bag or two of carrots and other miscellaneous vegetables.

But the game was up when the long arm of the law caught up with poachers Duggie, Ab and Nat after blood was spotted seeping from their stricken prey in their car while parked outside the Eagle and Child watering hole in deepest Rainford. Greenall and his countrified cohorts were cautioned, but released without charge after the estate's landowner, Lord Derby, had been informed. "I knew he would let us off because he was president of Saints and presented me with the Championship Cup in 1953," said Duggie. "But there was no chance that he would offer us jobs to allow us to become poachers-turned-gamekeepers."

Given the character that septuagenarian Duggie was, is, and always will be, stories about him abound, most of which are fact, a few fictional or maybe slightly embroidered. However, the following anecdote is, as they say in St Helens, 'gospel true:' Local decorators Critchley's, whose boss was Saints' director Rex Winter, were sprucing up The Engine and apprentice Geoff Heaton was told to strip the Greenall boudoir.

On entering the bedroom gob-smacked Geoff, now a Saints' Hall of Fame member, was astonished to find the happy couple still slumbering. "Carry on regardless," said Heaton's foreman, "Duggie and Vera won't wake up". And they didn't until the ceiling plaster fell in on them.

Time for tea! Alan Prescott, Tom van Vollenhoven , Eddie Bowden, Glyn Moses and Duggie Greenall after training at Knowsley Road in 1959.

Haven't we met somewhere before? Duggie Greenall and
Tom van Vollenhoven reminisce at Greenall's club in May 2006.
(Photo: Alex Service)

11. A flying Springbok

Ask any veteran Saints supporter what was the highlight of an otherwise uneventful 1957-58 season and the answer will be forthcoming in the blink of an eye - the arrival of Karel 'Tom' van Vollenhoven.

The signing of the South African rugby union wing ace rekindled the waning enthusiasm of fans yearning for a charismatic personality to be injected into a back line that was becoming hamstrung by a forward 'engine room' intent on a down-the-middle approach.

Again it was a case of cometh the hour cometh the man. For Saints were returning after defeating Liverpool City at Knotty Ash in October when Jim Sullivan snuggled up to Duggie on the coach and whispered "I know you are not happy with the way things went this afternoon, but not to worry, I'll have a brand new winger for you next week."

True to his word Sully introduced van Vollenhoven to the Saints side the following Tuesday and specifically instructed Greenall to put Tom through his paces regarding the rudiments of rugby league compared with rugby union, with particular emphasis on rule differences, positional play and tackling techniques.

"As I did with Steve Llewellyn 10 years earlier, Jim made it clear that I should nurse van Vollenhoven through his baptism in the professional code," recollected Duggie. "However, there was a slight problem when we began handling practice because Tom had difficulty holding the white plastic ball. So I thought it would be a good idea to try him with a coconut."

So, just six days after arriving in St Helens, the stage was set for South African Sportsman of the Year van Vollenhoven to wear the Saints' shirt for the first time against Leeds on Saturday 26 October before an ecstatic, albeit curious, 23,000 crowd. "I made him feel more at ease prior to the kick-off and told him the fans were all behind him," added streetwise Duggie.

The former Pretoria policeman had been lured to Saints in a cloak-and-dagger operation to ward off rivals Wigan. Fresh from his rugby union triumphs against the British Lions,

89

including a hat-trick in opposition to Irish legend Tony O'Reilly, the athletic 22-year-old van Vollenhoven was tailor-made for a wingman at 5 feet 10 inches and 12 stone.

Three tries Alex Murphy put Saints on the way to a 36-7 victory. The other scorers were Austin Rhodes with a try and six goals, Brian Howard, Ray Price and Duggie, before the one the restless fans had been praying for was delivered in majestic manner.

The final seconds were ticking away when Walter Delves, Greenall and Price split the Leeds defence to serve van Vollenhoven 40 yards out, and the flying Springbok outpaced George Broughton and Jimmy Dunn to cross at the scoreboard corner.

The Knowsley road faithful erupted on witnessing the first of the 392 tries notched in 409 games by van Vollenhoven for Saints, including the surpassing of Alf Ellaby's record of 55 in 1927, with Voll finishing on 62 in 1958-59.

Commenting in the *Reporter*, Tom Ashcroft stated that the South African had left no doubt over his try-scoring potential both in range and total - a study of van Vollenhoven's career would confirm the accuracy of that prophecy. As for Duggie he was in awe of the man after the final whistle: "His speed when going down the popular side was simply phenomenal - I was out of breath just watching him." exclaimed Greenall.

The teams on that red-letter day in Knowsley Road annals were:
St Helens: Glyn Moses; Tom van Vollenhoven, Duggie Greenall, Austin Rhodes, Brian Howard; Ray Price, Alex Murphy; Alan Prescott (capt.), Tom McKinney, Ab Terry, Nat Silcock, Walter Delves, Vince Karalius.
Leeds: Jimmy Dunn; Delmos Hodgkinson, Keith McLellan (capt.), Pat Quinn, George Broughton; Jack Lendill, Jeff Stevenson; David Skelton, Bernard Prior, Don Robinson, Arthur Tomlinson, Harry Street, Cliff Last.

Although the caring Duggie volunteered to keep Tom company on the field at Whitehaven the following week, Saints decided to leave van Vollenhoven in the 'A' team at home to the Cumbrians. The gate was a remarkable 8,000 and along with Tom, the threequarter line were all even-timer sprinters: Ken Large, Sammy Clemson and David

Johnson. The Springbok duly obliged with a brace of long-distance touchdowns - Voll had well and truly arrived.

Referring to the third-round Challenge Cup defeat at Featherstone later that season, Greenall chuckled: "That was the only dust-up I had with van Vollenhoven. I broke through in the closing minutes and signalled Tom to take my inside pass for a certain try under the posts, but he stayed on his wing and the chance went begging.

"When I gave him a piece of my mind he retorted 'don't you talk to me like that Greenall'. So I replied that I would ask our coach Jim Sullivan to switch me to the left wing alongside Frank Carlton in future. But Tom and I are still the best of pals."

Inevitably, van Vollenhoven was accorded a hero's welcome when he jetted over from Johannesburg for a whistle-stop tour of rugby league's heartlands in May 2006, with his fortnight-long holiday being sponsored by Warrington businessman Mike Donnison.

And no more eagerly was the red carpet rolled out than at Greenall's social club in St Helens, with hand-wringing, back-slapping banter being the order of the day when the van Vollenhoven-Greenall link was reforged in their first pow-wow since the millennium.

Greetings completed, these Saintly right-wing legends from 1957 then settled down to some highly amusing repartee which held the 200-strong audience spellbound. As did the questioning of Tom by compere Ray French, with the Springbok's illustrious career in union and league being the central theme.

Looking leaner than on his previous visit, the articulate van Vollenhoven pondered at length on how rugby league had changed since his day, in particular the virtual disappearance of the scrum, lack of running chances for wingers, and the marked increase in kicking. But he did concede that the game in general is faster and the players bigger.

Never a man to mince words, Duggie immediately countered: "Let's face it Tom, the game is not as good as when we played", a bone of contention that set the tempo for what proved to be a night to remember as Duggie and Tom held centre stage.

Globe-trotting van Vollenhoven was given a standing ovation when master-of-ceremonies French sounded the final hooter, and Tom was then besieged by hordes of autograph and photograph-hunting fans, which found him burning the midnight oil in a bid to meet their requests.

Duggie, meanwhile, ensured that the amber liquid continued to flow for the dynamic duo, which was totally par for the course for these giants of yesteryear not averse to a drop of 'shoulder ale' from besotted Saints supporters.

However the last word rested with van Vollenhoven when he intriguingly remarked that, such was his affection for St Helens and its people, he might consider settling in the town - a suggestion guaranteed to setting tongues wagging both in the borough and far beyond.

The arrival of the legendary van Vollenhoven apart, Saints' second successive trophy-less campaign put them under the microscope, in the wake of the euphoria of their Challenge Cup conquest of Halifax at Wembley Stadium in 1956.

Their Lancashire Cup aspirations were dashed yet again by Oldham, this time by 29-9 in the semi-final at Knowsley Road. "Saints' defeat was of shock dimensions because we fancied our chances of avenging Oldham's victory in the final the previous season," said Duggie. "However it should be remembered that the Roughyeds were league champions and were bristling with talent, including the likes of Alan Davies, Frank Pitchford and Derek Turner, and Saints could only manage a late try from Nat Silcock."

Challenge Cup dreams were shattered via that loudly lamented reverse in the blizzard that enveloped Featherstone's inhospitable Post Office Road, with fate decreeing a similar tragedy for Saints during the following season on a pitch which became known as the 'graveyard' to all at Knowsley Road.

Saints finished runners-up to Oldham in the league table with 64 points from 38 games, only to lose by a nail-biting 14-13 against Workington in the top-four play-off. "It was sickening," said Duggie who was by then on the wrong side of 30, "because one season without silverware is one thing, but two - perish the thought."

Despite the trophy cupboard remaining bare Saints provided a record six players for the 1958 tour of Australia and New Zealand. They were Great Britain captain Alan Prescott, Ab Terry, Frank Carlton, Glyn Moses, Vince Karalius and 18-years-old Alex Murphy, buoyed by scoring 27 tries for Saints in his first full season.

And Saints' representation to the Antipodes might have numbered seven, because Duggie was asked about his willingness to make a second consecutive trip. Duggie explained: "Saints' director Jim Yearsley was a member of the selection committee and I was flattered when he approached me. But injuries and general wear-and-tear were beginning to take their toll and I had to refuse Mr Yearsley after discussing the matter with my wife Vera."

With Duggie an icon among the Knowsley Road supporters it might be pertinent at this point to solicit the opinion of a well-known figure on the terraces when Duggie was strutting his stuff in earnest. Like Duggie, senior citizen and lifelong Saints supporter Jack Coatsworth merited legend status at Knowsley Road, but for rather different reasons than Duggie.

For while feats of derring-do on the field were Duggie's forte, it was charismatic back-room boy Coatsworth's dressing room activities which brought him fame at Saints, as did his regular distribution of Everton Mints to the players which found him dubbed 'Toffee Jack'.

Unswerving in his admiration of Duggie's uncompromising approach to the hurly-burly of rugby league, Jack said: "Dad first took me to Knowsley Road in my short-pants days in 1936 and I remain a regular to this day. I have been privileged to watch many Saints greats, and I am of the opinion that each and every one of them will be remembered for their personal skills and characteristics. In this respect Duggie was famous for his devastating crash-tackling and for protecting his wingman. He first wore the Saints' shirt with pride as a callow youth of 17, when his rugby mentor was Harry Cook.

"Duggie appeared in every back position before finding his true niche in the centre. When Steve Llewellyn arrived from South Wales Duggie took him under his wing (no pun intended) and helped him adapt to rugby league. And when Tom van Vollenhoven jetted over from South Africa nine years later Duggie gave action replays of his virtuoso centre displays by having a major role in Tom's prolific try-scoring sprees.

"Duggie knew no fear in demolishing his opposite number with a tackle timed to perfection, and even though his opponent was usually much heavier than the pencil-slim Duggie the magic sponge was often needed to revive the unwary victim.

"Defeat by Huddersfield at Wembley in 1953 was a bitter disappointment to everyone at Saints, Duggie in particular. But he made a solemn vow to the fans that the team would bring back the Championship Cup a fortnight later. That was no empty promise as Saints romped home against Halifax.

"Tales of 'war' with the Australians, impromptu renderings of *Mammy* and the fictional plaster cast, are all entrenched in the folk-lore figure that is Duggie Greenall, as were his green-fingered skills in growing onions the size of rugby balls in his postage-stamp garden just a drop-kick from Knowsley Road in Doulton Street."

12. Championship encore

Following two barren seasons Saints bounced back onto the trophy trail in 1958-59, but had to wait until the final game of the campaign to get their hands on the League Championship trophy at last.

Always regarded as an accurate barometer of a season's work, that particular pot arrived with the 44-22 defeat of Hunslet at Odsal Stadium and came in the wake of a period which had witnessed a shift in both players and captaincy, the latter albeit temporarily.

A study of the season reveals that injuries on the summer tour of Australia sustained by Alan Prescott to his arm and Glyn Moses to his knee meant that both faced long absences, and with this in mind Saints reappointed the tried-and-trusted Duggie as skipper.

Incoming stars included second-rowers Dick Huddart, Brian Briggs and Jimmy Measures, South African winger Jan Prinsloo and centre Ken Large, while 'Mr Dependable' Wilf Smith was forging a formidable half-back link with Alex Murphy, and teenager Brian McGinn was also making his presence felt in the back division.

Goalkicking utility back Peter Fearis deputised initially for the limping Moses before being supplanted by Austin Rhodes, who later made the full-back spot his own. Up front Nat Silcock and Ab Terry alternated in the number eight jersey for Prescott, whose fractured arm was proving slow to heal.

Commenting on this time of transition at Knowsley Road when he was in his 32nd year, Duggie said: "Although I was sorry for Prescott and Moses having bad luck on tour, I was nevertheless thrilled to be handed the captaincy once more because I did not want to lose it in the first place.

"Despite Saints losing their opening game at Widnes I remember thinking we were due for a good season because of the important signings that had been made, especially that of Dick Huddart, who had been outstanding for Whitehaven against Saints at the Recreation Ground."

Duggie's words of wisdom proved prophetic - if only in the league competition - for Saints topped the table with 63 points from 38 games, in the process of which they really cut loose in amassing a record 1,005 points in tries and goals.

However, it was a rather different tale in sudden death Cup warfare, because Saints were defeated 12-2 by Oldham in the Lancashire Cup Final at Swinton, and then bowed out of the Challenge Cup for a second successive year at windswept Post Office Road, Featherstone, this time to the tune of 20-6.

The teams for the Lancashire Cup Final were:

Oldham: B. Ganley; R. Cracknell, A. Davies, J. Noon, J. Etty; A. Kellett, F. Pitchford; R. Rowbottom, J. Keith, K. Jackson, C. Winslade, D. McKeown, D. Turner.
Scorers: Tries: Davies, Kellett. Goals: Ganley (2), Kellett.
St Helens: P. Fearis, T. van Vollenhoven, D. Greenall, K. Large, F. Carlton, B. Howard, A. Murphy; A. Terry, T. McKinney, D. Brown, B. Briggs, W. Delves, V. Karalius.
Scorer: Goal: Fearis.

Without doubt the individual highlight of 1958-59 was the setting of a new St Helens try-scoring record of 62 in 45 games by the incomparable Tom van Vollenhoven, with the previous best being 55 by fellow legend Alf Ellaby in 1927. Voll's tally included eight hat-tricks and, when it is remembered that his centre Duggie notched 21 touchdowns it will be readily understood why this lethal right-wing partnership is etched indelibly into Saints' folklore.

Greenall lined up alongside van Vollenhoven in more than 70 games in less than three seasons, and certainly did more than his bit in blooding Tom into the rigours of rugby league, in particular because wingers saw more of the ball and were required to tackle more often than in rugby union.

Duggie outlined: "I can vividly recall the roar of expectancy when the ball moved across Saints' threequarter line towards van Vollenhoven, because the crowd had grown to expect something out of the ordinary and Tom usually came up with just that.

"Quite simply the man had everything: lightning speed, baffling swerve and sidestep, uncanny change of direction and pace, a sledgehammer hand-off and - once settled into the rugby league code - a tremendous tackling technique especially when covering on the opposite wing.

"Tom's fellow Springbok Jan Prinsloo was a big, upstanding winger who often dived in the act of scoring, a ploy which brought him several of his 27 tries that season. However, I always felt that Jan was unlucky in having to live within the shadow of the peerless van Vollenhoven."

Both van Vollenhoven and Prinsloo were destined to parade their prolific scoring talents before discerning patrons of the newly built main stand in 1958. Constructed by local firms Yearsleys and Todds, who were represented on Saints' board, and designed to seat 2,300, the structure cost £32,000 and Duggie believes that it should be christened the 'Tom van Vollenhoven Stand' as a tribute to the 392-try maestro.

Christmas 1958 was certainly a testing time for Saints for they played three games in as many days. They won 10-6 at Leigh on Christmas Day, then beat Wigan 13-9 at Knowsley Road on Boxing Day and then walloped visitors Oldham 22-6. Duggie appeared in all three, as did Glyn Moses, Tom van Vollenhoven, Jan Prinsloo, Ab Terry, Dick Huddart and Vince Karalius. That speaks volumes for their fitness and stamina in those distant days.

As the Championship season gathered momentum and Saints moved inexorably to pole position, stand-in skipper Duggie was not best pleased when the Saints leadership reverted to the now-recovering Prescott. "I was poised to set another record after being Saints' skipper against Halifax in 1953 but it was not to be, so I soldiered on determined to do my best for Preccy, and enjoyed the great consolation of a second Championship medal," remarked Duggie.

A thigh strain kept van Vollenhoven out of the top-four play-off when Saints trounced Oldham 42-4 at Knowsley Road. Tom's deputy Ken Large scored a hat-trick after Duggie did much of the spadework but, in view of what happened a fortnight hence at Odsal, it was just as well that van Vollenhoven was declared fit to play.

Outsiders Hunslet - who qualified by overcoming Challenge Cup holders Wigan 22-11 at Central Park - gave their supporters in the 52,560 crowd an early boost in building up a 12-4 lead courtesy of tries by Jim Stockdill and Kevin Doyle, plus three goals from Billy Langton. Slow-to-start Saints could manage only two penalties by Rhodes and, with 12 minutes gone, disenchanted Saints' fans were venting their feelings saying "you've let us down again".

But not for much longer, for, with Saints' looking towards heaven in search of divine inspiration, that man van Vollenhoven delivered it with a top-drawer try ranking among the greatest ever scored, and crucial in that it brought struggling Saints back into serious contention.

Knee-deep in nostalgia, Duggie took up the sensational story: "It's now 47 years ago but, as with the rest of the Saints side, I was not at my best when I threw out a long speculative pass to van Vollenhoven, who was near the touchline with 75 yards to go to the Hunslet try-line.

Somehow he jinked past his opposite number Willie Walker - who had been instructed to 'police' Tom - then he held off Preece, Doyle and Shaw with an incredible change of pace, and handed off Langton, while my last sighting of the vanishing Voll being as he turned in for the posts with Don Hatfield trailing in his slipstream."

Rhodes tacked on the conversion and then added a penalty to leave Saints just 12-11 in arrears on the half-hour. The Knowsley Road team were now in total command as Murphy, Prinsloo and van Vollenhoven again, from a Duggie back-pass, crossed the Hunslet line to forge into a convincing 24-12 half-time lead.

Van Vollenhoven completed his hat-trick on the restart, with the other Saints tries being notched by Murphy again, Smith and Huddart, and Rhodes established another Championship Final record in landing 10 goals. The Parksiders' second-half touchdowns came from Poole and Gunney, and Langton ended with five goals.

Van Vollenhoven was carried shoulder-high from the dusty Odsal bowl by ecstatic fans, and there was an encore performance of euphoric welcome for the Saints conquering heroes in Victoria Square on that unforgettable Saturday, 16 May 1959.

As for the veteran Duggie, he was according a rapturous ovation from the milling throng when introduced by Saints' chairman Harry Cook who said: "Duggie has been given a new lease of life with the signing of van Vollenhoven and led Saints magnificently during the enforced absence of Prescott."

Fittingly, given his father and son relationship with coach Jim Sullivan, Duggie later presented his mentor with an inscribed gold watch on behalf of the Saints' squad. 'Sully' was leaving for Rochdale Hornets following seven seasons of soaring success at Knowsley Road.

The teams on that wonderful day in Saints' history were:

St Helens: Austin Rhodes; Tom Van Vollenhoven, Duggie Greenall, Brian McGinn, Jan Prinsloo; Wilf Smith, Alex Murphy; Alan Prescott (capt.), Tom McKinney, Ab Terry, Brian Briggs, Dick Huddart, Vince Karalius.

Hunslet: Billy Langton; Ron Colin, Jim Stockdill, Alan Preece, Willie Walker; Brian Gabbitas, Kevin Doyle; Don Hatfield, Sam Smith, Ken Eyre, Harry Poole, Geoff Gunney, Brian Shaw.

As in 1950, champions Saints then embarked on a week-long tour of South Wales to spread the rugby league gospel, during which they won all three games at Cardiff, Bridgend and Ystradgynlais. Pint-pulling at The Engine meant Greenall travelled to Wales on the following Monday and, after playing in two matches, he then took Jan Prinsloo on a sight-seeing trip to London for the first time.

THE NORTHERN RUGBY FOOTBALL LEAGUE

League Championship Final
1959

HUNSLET v. ST. HELENS

SATURDAY
16th MAY
1959

Kick-off 3.0 p.m.

At ODSAL STADIUM
BRADFORD

OFFICIAL SOUVENIR PROGRAMME - Price 6d.

GIDEON SHAW, PRINTER, CASTLEFORD

The programme from St Helens' third League Championship, secured with
a brilliant 44-22 win over the men from Parkside in 1959.
(Courtesy RFL)

Duggie Greenall is challenged by Hunslet winger Willie Walker as he sends Tom van Vollenhoven in for his second try in the Championship Final.
(Photo: Courtesy Robert Gate)

Some of the St Helens team that won the title. Left to right: Brian McGinn, Wilf Smith, Duggie Greenall, Brian Briggs, Austin Rhodes, Tom van Vollenhoven, Dick Huddart, Alex Murphy, Ab Terry and coach Jim Sullivan.

Duggie Greenall, Jim Sullivan and Tom van Vollenhoven with the
Championship Trophy at Odsal in 1959.

South Africans Tom van Vollenhoven and Jan Prinsloo team up with
Duggie Greenall in a bout of handling practice at Knowsley Road in 1959.
(Photo: Courtesy Robert Gate)

13. A fond farewell

A 14-season love affair with Saints that blossomed after the Second World War was destined to end for the grieving Duggie in 1959-60, a period in which newly-appointed coach Alan Prescott's side revealed themselves as being of a Jekyll and Hyde personality.

Saints started the campaign like the proverbial house on fire by winning their opening 13 games but, as will be revealed in due course, they ended the season empty-handed save for the Lancashire League Trophy. The first defeat came at the hands of Australia by 15-2, when Duggie was left out with his previous flare-ups with the tourists having a profound bearing on his omission.

A reflective Duggie said: "I was included in the squad but it was then I began to feel that I was not wanted at Knowsley Road. The board's view was that I had to make way for the faster Ken Large because it was felt that I was losing my pace over a distance.

"I soldiered on to regain my place and was named in the Saints side which lost by a cliffhanging 5-4 to Warrington in the Lancashire Cup Final at Central Park, Wigan. But I swear to this day that Saints were robbed by a hotly-disputed try by Brian Bevan, who did not appear to touch down a chip-through to the corner by St. Helens-born Bobby Greenough.

"Maybe the fact Saints wore unfamiliar black and white jerseys was an omen of disaster to come, while the fact that Vince Karalius cried off at the last minute did nothing to help our cause as Warrington won the Lancashire Cup for the first time since 1937."

A galling defeat to be sure for suffering Saints following a match which remained pointless throughout the second half, and watched by a terrace-packing crowd of 39,237 on a grey October afternoon in 1959 when Duggie was fated to appear in his last big occasion for the club. The teams were:

Warrington: Eric Fraser; Brian Bevan, Jim Challinor, Laurie Gilfedder, Terry O'Grady; Bobby Greenough, Jackie Edwards; Nat Silcock, Pat Lannon, Alistair Brindle, Jack Arkwright, Harry Major, Albert Naughton (capt.).

Scorers: Try: Bevan. Goal: Fraser.

St Helens: Austin Rhodes; Tom van Vollenhoven, Duggie Greenall, Brian McGinn, Jan Prinsloo; Wilf Smith, Alex Murphy; Ab Terry, Tom McKinney, Alan Prescott (capt.), Brian Briggs, Dick Huddart, Fred Terry.
Scorer: Goals: Rhodes (2).

"I appeared in only a handful of matches before my last against Workington at Knowsley Road on 5 December, when Saints were beaten 12-11. After that I was transfer-listed at what Saints believed was a realistic fee of £5,000," said Duggie. "I 'scriked' my eyes out when I got back to The Engine, because all that I ever wanted to do was play for the club right from the day I signed from the Air Training Corps."

However, the loyalty of battle-hardened veteran Duggie was recognised by grateful Saints, who presented him with an inscribed gold watch in tribute to his astonishing courage and devotion to both team and club. Chairman Harry Cook had previously told Duggie to choose a suitable timepiece so, Duggie being Duggie, he went to local up-market jewellers Watkinson's and emerged with the most expensive in the shop. It was inscribed "Presented to Duggie Greenall by Saints' directors for loyal and devoted service 1944-60".

After topping the table for a second successive season with 34 victories in 38 games Saints were beaten 19-9 by Wigan in the top-four play-off at Knowsley Road, on a day when stand-offs Alex Murphy and Mick Sullivan were sent off following a bout of fisticuffs. Tom van Vollenhoven headed the league scorers' chart with 54 tries, half of which came when Greenall was inside him, while Austin Rhodes topped the goalkickers with 171.

Challenge Cup hopes were dashed when Wakefield Trinity triumphed 15-10 at Knowsley Road and, with silverware dreams shattered all this led to a demand from fans for a return to the fold for the departed Duggie, which was a classic case of shutting the stable door after the horse had reluctantly bolted.

Given he was nigh on 33 years old, a now footloose-and-fancy-free Duggie had been flattered by the interest shown by several top clubs, notably Wigan, Warrington, Leeds and Widnes. Despite tacit pressure from the Knowsley Road hierarchy and supporters, he hit the Central Park trail, after uttering words of consolation that he was only going on a spying mission for his beloved Saints.

Perhaps due to dyed-in-the-wool rivalry between Saints and Wigan, Duggie never settled in a cherry and white jersey. "Few players spoke to me or passed to me in training moves," he remembered. "I gained the impression that I was being sent to Coventry, and Norman Cherrington was the only true friend I made at Central Park.

"I reckon that I appeared in no more than four games for Wigan, and that included captaining the 'A' team at Rochdale when we won 9-8, where I rescued Wigan with a try-saving tackle in the final minute. The dressing room door was flung open and in stormed Hornets coach Jim Sullivan shouting 'you've done us again Greenall', all in fun, of course."

The parting of the ways for Duggie and Wigan came when he failed to report for training, which resulted in a letter from the club stating that, until he re-appeared, Greenall would not be considered for selection in either first or reserve team games - it was time to move on again.

Duggie's brief stay at Central Park was not without incidents both hilarious and otherwise, as one can imagine. In particular, he recalls a trip to the seaside with Mick Sullivan for the game versus Blackpool Borough at the St Anne's Road stadium.

"Sully asked me for a lift," remembered Duggie. "There was no motorway then and I must have taken a wrong turning because we got lost. I was stopped by the police for speeding when trying to make up for lost time, and when we arrived at the ground the game had been postponed due to bad weather. I think Mick was glad to get out of the car because it had certainly been a hair-raising ride."

On again now for the itinerant Duggie, this time to Odsal Stadium, Bradford, where Northern handed him the player-coach role at a club struggling in the lower reaches of the league table, with low gates, lack of money and shortage of team spirit being inevitable consequences.

"As at Wigan, I stuck it out for a month or so before getting fed-up of the 150-mile round trip into Yorkshire," Duggie recollected, "and after getting home to The Engine, which Vera was running single-handed, at midnight from Hull I told Bradford that enough was enough.

"They were very understanding and offered to find me other pubs in Bradford, Huddersfield and Halifax but my mind was made up, and when I thought about the whole affair I realised that I was set in my ways following a lifetime at Saints, and I should have hung up my boots there and then."

However, never being one to refuse a friend, Duggie couldn't resist the temptation when former Saints team-mate and Liverpool City chairman Bill Whittaker asked him to take charge of training at their Knotty Ash ground. "They had little money, gates were numbered in hundreds and the pitch was often like a ploughed field but the enthusiasm for rugby league knew no bounds even though they won just five games out of 36," he recalled.

"The lack of resources was brought home to me at a training session when I told a director that the players had just one rugby ball to pass around, and a tatty one at that. 'Not to worry,' came the reply, 'I'll soon fix that,' and he quickly returned with half-a-dozen of the soccer variety which he had borrowed from a Huyton junior side."

With professional rugby league cares now behind him, it was time for Duggie to concentrate fully on the family bread-and-butter at The Engine watering hole, be it tapping barrels and cleaning pumps, or even the more mundane tasks of polishing glasses and hostelry artefacts.

Having said that, Duggie was not averse to the odd game of tick-and-pass with well-practised elbow-benders on what was once The Engine bowling green and, in their turn, his thirsty clients also wallowed in the buzz of rubbing shoulders with a rugby league icon whose name was a household one from Barrow to Brisbane.

He now had the opportunity for a moment or two for reflection on his teenage years during the Second World War, which found the grateful Duggie eternally mindful of the sacrifices made in the cause of freedom, in particular that of former Parr Central School scrum-half Harold Briscoe, who gave his life on the last day of the conflict.

In this respect Duggie has made several pilgrimages to the battlefields of the Somme, the sounding of the *Last Post* at Ypres, and the beaches of Normandy so redolent of the liberation of Europe in the dark and dangerous days of 1944.

Elsewhere, there was nothing that golf-widow Vera Greenall enjoyed more than to see club-wielding Duggie jetting off to far-flung courses such as in Portugal and Spain, or up the road at Bowring Park, Liverpool, and Ashton-in-Makerfield.

All this was in tandem with such other lovers of the links as the late Jack Manley, Frank Phillips and Denis McLoughlin - like Duggie all one-time purveyors of the life-giving fluid that flowed from Greenall Whitley Brewery.

Sting-in-the-golfing tale for Duggie came at the Engine, on a glorious afternoon in the 1950s, when on checking the till he found there had been no customers. "I might as well go for a round of golf," he told Vera. Imagine his surprise on discovering that the front door of the pub had remained locked since the night before.

Saying a fond farewell to the sharp end of rugby league had proved quite a culture shock for Duggie, but he remained philosophical in reminding himself that time and tide wait for no man. "The regular slurpers of Derbyshire Hill and Newton Road kept me busy manning the pumps at The Engine, and in this respect I was grateful for the help of 'our Ve' and my dad Ted," remembered the likeable landlord.

"However we still managed to squeeze in trips to our favourite holiday hideaway at Villa Del Mar, Benidorm, where my wife and I would escape the winter by soaking up the sun, often for as long as three weeks. Word of my rugby league background spread like wildfire both in our 'digs' and around the place, and I was buttonholed daily by holidaymakers and locals alike asking 'Are you the Duggie Greenall from St Helens?'

"Then came constant requests for autographs and photographs from hordes of people, many of whom readily admitted that they had only seen rugby league on the telly. I could only think that my reputation had gone before me through the radio and press because, apart from the occasional clip, television coverage was limited in my day."

Having regaled his new-found fan club with deeds of derring-do both on and off the field, the garrulous Duggie could honestly say that he had done more for Anglo-Spanish relations than many a diplomat, and was often asked 'When are you going to write a book on your exploits abroad and in the rugby league heartlands?' Duggie was asked the same question by his relations in America, Ian and Susan Campbell. Duggie and Vera maintain a trans-Atlantic link with them in Atlanta and Illinois.

Another less pleasant memory from when he had retired from the game came in 1963, when Duggie rocked a police surgeon back on his heels from the dock of a Liverpool Court.

The former Saints' star was appearing on a charge of drunken driving, swerving all over the road and mounting the pavement four times. The judge told Duggie that he had considered sending him to prison, but decided to take a more lenient view by banning him from driving for 12 months.

When the surgeon asked him if he had ever been injured, the defendant rattled off a list that sounded like a casualty call on a night in the London blitz: a broken jaw, a dislocated shoulder, two broken legs, two broken ankles, nose broken five times, a fractured skull, black eyes, facial displacements, countless head stitches, four broken ribs and double vision in both eyes.

Then Duggie asked: "Is that enough to be going on with? There's more if you want it. I've had suspected skull and jaw fractures, and I don't know how many x-rays for suspected broken legs and ribs in Australia." Some of the broken legs and ribs in Australia on the 1954 tour may not have been his.

Eight years of happy, if sometimes chequered, stewardship at The Engine saw Duggie finally calling 'time, gentlemen please' in 1964, when both he and Vera felt the need to move on, on this occasion to the Talbot Hotel in town-centre Duke Street. Nowadays dubbed The Sportsman and boasting a reproduction of a rugby player on its facade, this time-honoured oasis of good cheer saw Duggie Greenall holding the licence for the next decade, in the course of which the popular pub developed a certain ambience and, much to the brewery's delight, a steady increase in takings.

Even after he retired, Duggie's status in the town remained very high. He and Vera were once at the back of the queue at the Capitol cinema, Duke Street, when the blockbuster film *The Magnificent Seven* was showing. But they were not bringing up the rear for long, for the doorman - a Saints' fan - ushered them to the best seats free of charge. No other patron objected, such was the popularity of the Greenalls among St Helens folk.

Unforeseen illness intervened in 1975, when a hitherto fit-as-a-fiddle Duggie contracted tuberculosis and was admitted to Eccleston Hall Sanatorium, just a drop-kick away from the scene of his many triumphs at Knowsley Road.

He was confined to the isolation ward for three weeks before the streptomycin antibiotic got him back on his feet. With visiting restrictions now lifted Duggie rejoiced in his greater freedom, but this brought problems because he was inundated by well-wishers, and the subsequent banter was scarcely conducive to hospital tranquillity.

Added to all this was a marked tendency for the gregarious Duggie to be smitten by wanderlust, which found him encroaching into wards reserved for cancer patients, including old-time Saints, St Helens Recs and Great Britain forward Albert Fildes. "Get out Mr Greenall, you might infect them," bellowed a rather starchy matron, as red-faced Duggie tried to explain that he was only offering a friendly word of comfort.

Convalescence followed in the Canary Isles and a rejuvenated Duggie returned to the bitter and mild life behind the bar at The Talbot. That was until 1984 when Boddington's Brewery, who were involved in a take-over from Greenall Whitley, offered to sell Duggie the pub for £20,000.

"There was no way that I could raise that kind of money," said a crestfallen Duggie. "But they could not put us out on the street so, after much argy-bargy, Boddington's came up with a compromise in offering me The Surrey Arms in Glossop. Vera and I reluctantly decided to give it a go. However we quickly realised that, being in an area foreign to rugby league fans, it was just not our scene even though the previous landlord was a former Salford player, whose name escapes me.

"By and large the up-market clientele were gin-and-tonic, half-a-bitter types, often to be found in the lavishly appointed cocktail bar and lounge. Football was their main sporting topic, and customers regularly took the road south to support either Sheffield Wednesday or United. And the fact that there was a long-established hotel opposite The Surrey Arms obviously had its effect on our bar profits.

"The wife and I were approaching middle age and decided to put our spell in Derbyshire down to experience," went on a greatly relieved Duggie, "So we packed our bags, upped sticks and headed for good old St Helens, and we will always treasure the welcome home greetings that were showered on us. On settling in 109 Doulton Street I can remember thinking that I had been a publican for more than 30 years - enough is enough you might say. It also crossed my mind that no Saints player had ever been in any of my four pubs except decorator Geoff Heaton. "Did I have BO?" wondered Duggie.

When viewing the cosy terraced house Duggie quickly spotted an uncultivated garden area of postage-stamp dimensions. A frustrated man-of-the-soil throughout the previous generation, a now green-fingered Duggie set to work with abandon to grow king-size onions, tasty tomatoes and eye-catching blooms. He was so successful that prospective purchasers beat a path to his door, including former *St Helens Star* editor Alan Whalley, who penned several highly complimentary features on the fruits of Duggie's digging and delving within the confines of his back yard at number 109.

A few streets in St Helens bear names with a Saintly ring, notably Prescot Road, Parr Street, Ellaby Road and Frodsham Drive, but any link to oval ball heroes is purely coincidental. However, on this theme, Douglas Street and Greenall Street are in Duggie's parish to this day, but he was at pains to point out that they were built long before he rocketed to fame with the Saints. Nonetheless, he feels strongly that some kind of gesture should be in place as a tribute to Tom van Vollenhoven, be it statue, street, stand or similar edifice.

The ongoing construction of supermarkets has led to a new lease of life for Mr and Mrs Greenall in their retirement years. They can often be spotted in Morrisons, Tesco, Asda and Ikea in Burtonwood, where Duggie finds the restaurant's meatballs drenched in gravy irresistible.

Vera makes light of her current mobility problems in skilfully negotiating the food isles in a state-of-the-art electric wheelchair, but there is no such luxury for her devoted hubby, who can be spotted loading goodies into a manually propelled trolley, in particular at the delicatessen and fish counters, where cockles, mussels and whelks are selected with great discernment.

Financial disaster almost struck on one visit to Morrisons following confusion at the check-out when Vera's handbag went astray, with the loss only being discovered when the distressed couple arrived home. Panic reigned because the bag contained several hundred pounds, but their worries were short-lived when a Saints supporter returned it to them intact after finding it in the trolley park and noting the name of the owner. Superfluous to say, a grateful Mrs Greenall ensured that his honesty was suitably rewarded.

A quintessential 'Sintelliner' from the tip of his sometimes aching toes to his thickly-thatched greying head, a durable Duggie now in his 80th year is of somewhat wider girth than of yore, 17 stones in fact. His medication means he takes a dozen tablets daily, four inhalers (he calls them puffers), has the odd denture or so - blame that on rugby - and monthly trips to the chiropodist. Despite being at the sharp end of the toughest game in the sporting pantheon, Duggie still has most of his natural teeth.

Despite these apparent ravages of time, Duggie has still emerged relatively unscathed from a wholly demanding rugby league odyssey in that he does not sport the once-trademark cauliflower ears, misshapen nose or other facial scars of battle. What you see is what you get with Duggie: ruddy countenance, mischievous grin, puckish wit, firm handshake and an inbuilt willingness to chew the rugby league cud with all and sundry. Duggie has all these attributes in abundance and more besides.

Wisely, perhaps, given the passing years, Duggie and his beloved Vera left Doulton Street in 2002 to live with son Douglas and his wife Jean in tree-lined residential Windle. When assembled, the Greenall family circle is numerous to say the least because it also comprises grandchildren Lee, Amanda, Wendy, Gemma, Natalie, Christopher; great-grandchildren Bethany, Connor, Jamie-Lee and Tyler. Add to that spouses and partners and it will be understood that the family Christmas dinner table is a tight squeeze indeed.

Famous five: Left to right Glyn Moses, Steve Llewellyn, Duggie Greenall, Don Gullick, Stan McCormick. They formed the Saints' back division at Wembley in 1953 and in the Championship win against Halifax a fortnight later. They were attending the Past Players' dinner in 1993.
(Photo: Alex Service)

Duggie Greenall, Jimmy Stott and Alan Prescott out for a stroll when Saints and Huddersfield toured South Wales in 1949.

Seconds out! Duggie Greenall and Tom van Vollenhoven delighted these youngsters of Lowe House boxing club when they ducked under the ropes at Halefield Street in 1978.

"I don't speak to Wiganers!" was Duggie Greenall's opening gambit to an amused Maurice Lindsay (beneath the microphone) at the Past Players' Association dinner at Knowsley Road in 1998.

Duggie Greenall and George Parr in party mood at the Past Players
Association annual dinner in 2003.
(Photo: Alex Service)

Doting grand-dad Duggie Greenall with Amanda and Lee at the rear of
the Talbot Hotel, Duke Street, where he was the legendary landlord.

14. Then and now

Predictably, given the 47-year time scale since hanging up his boots, Duggie has some pretty strong views on the way rugby league has changed since his heyday. "I remember Tom van Vollenhoven remarking on this at the Saints' Centenary match against the Australians in 1990," said Duggie. "The first thing Tom said was what he had just seen was not the game he played for Saints from 1957. What would he think 16 years later?"

Certainly rugby league has undergone a radical facelift, much of it necessary to meet the challenge of modern times, and Duggie highlights just a few facets of the game that have affected its pattern over the past decade. These include scrums becoming effectively redundant with the hooking role now merely the acting half-back. He notes that forwards do not push for the ball, so scrummaging is now a farce because possession invariably goes to the side with head and feed. "It's just another way of re-starting play in a bid to speed up the game," declared Duggie.

Another change is the six-tackle rule, initially four-tackles, which was brought in to prevent sides monopolising the ball and hopefully open out play. But this has led to charges that the pattern of rugby league nowadays is one of five drives and a kick. Hence his belief that our code is more like rugby union than ever.

The try now counts four points instead of three. A drop-goal is one point instead of the previous two. This was justified in order to reflect the true value of a try to that of a drop-goal.

We have summer rugby and with it full-time professionalism and saturation coverage of Super League on Sky Television, which appears to be the Holy Grail of the rugby league hierarchy. This is because of the massive input of Sky TV money. Time-honoured clubs such as Dewsbury, Halifax, Oldham and Swinton now appear to be among the game's poor relations.

Substitutes, video referees, fourth officials and the like are now the norm, which is understandable because the game is admittedly faster than in Duggie's career. More innovations include the sin-bin, blood-bin and referees placing players on report, with sendings-off almost just a memory.

All this might lead one to think that Duggie is not enamoured with modern-day rugby league, and to a certain extent that would be correct. But he readily concedes that today's players are super-fit athletes, with beer bellies conspicuous by their absence, as are cauliflower ears and misshapen features which have become things of the past, due to the purge on head-high tackles.

However, Duggie is sad that the days of 50-plus tries in a season by a winger such as Tom van Vollenhoven or Billy Boston seem to have disappeared. Obviously there are reasons for this, not least the manner in which rugby league has evolved during the past 10 years or so. But Duggie remains convinced that fans like nothing better than to see a winger in full flight for the line.

And to further illustrate the changing face of our game he revealed that Saints' legendary coach of the 1950s Jim Sullivan operated a no-kicking policy at Knowsley Road, this at a time when, like today, the team was riding high. "Sully's opinion was that if your side had the ball the opposition could not score," recalled Duggie. "I can remember one remarkable incident when Austin Rhodes chipped through for van Vollenhoven to touch down. But, far from being happy, Sullivan's response to Rhodes was 'do that again and you will be dropped next week.' Jim believed that rugby league was first and foremost a handling and running game."

Duggie's view of Super League is that although it boasts 12 teams, in reality it is a competition dominated by the big four of Saints, Leeds, Bradford and Wigan, even though the last named struggled in the 2006 season. "Saints supporters might take issue with me," chuckled Duggie, "but I believe that rugby league needs a strong Wigan because they are one of the bastions of the game and a household name throughout the world."

Duggie's mobility problems mean that oval ball viewing is mainly confined to television these days as he enters his 80s. However, wild horses would not keep him away from the Past Players' Annual Dinner at Knowsley Road, when a rapturous welcome is guaranteed for one of Saints' most unforgettable characters.

Lest we forget, it could be said that Duggie was a chip of the old block because his dad Ned was an all-action forward with amateur side Gerard's Bridge Rovers in the 1920s. He later signed for St Helens Recs, but did not appear in the first team due to the dominance of legendary back three Smith, Fildes and Mulvanney. Duggie recalled: "Dad never complimented me on my progress in rugby league, perhaps he was jealous. But woe betide anyone who 'knocked' me to him. Then the fur would really fly."

Duggie's rafter-raising rendition of *Mammy* on Sky Television's *Boots 'n All* in 2005 proved to be a big hit both with the audience and presenters Bill Arthur and Dave Hadfield. It was delivered *al fresco* from Duggie's garden in deepest Windle, where the clothes line and other impedimenta had to be removed for visual and acoustic reasons.

It was not, however, Duggie's debut before the television cameras because he appeared on a Granada sports programme, along with soccer's Bill Shankly and Denis Law, who were then with Huddersfield Town. "We got a tanner a mile travel expenses which meant we all pocketed the princely sum of 30 measly bob [£1.50]" remembered a rueful Duggie.

Duggie was a hilarious after-dinner speaker, but also rendered deeply touching eulogies at the funerals of team-mates Steve Llewellyn, Stan McCormick, George Parr and Alan Prescott. He is the sole survivor of the celebrated threequarter line of Llewellyn, Greenall, Gullick and McCormick, each of whom were automatic choices at Saints in the glory days of the early 1950s.

In retrospect the impact, both literally and metaphorically, that Greenall had on the Kangaroos in the 1950s is now the stuff of legends. This was further epitomised by a *Daily Express* report after Saints played the Australians at Knowsley Road in the Centenary season of 1990.

In a story headlined 'Tough guys are a league apart' sports editor James Lawton wrote: "No one really knows who quite lit the torch which has blazed so brilliantly throughout the Rugby League Ashes series, but we could do worse than start with Duggie Greenall.

"A granite-hard centre for Great Britain back in the 1950s, 63-year-old Duggie stepped up to the biggest Aussie at the reception and recalled his only tour of 1954. Gently prodding the giant chest, 5 feet 9 inches, (playing weight 11 stones) Greenall declared 'I laid on thee feyther then, and I'll lay on thee naw if tha wants.' A rather amused police officer stepped in to prevent a possible breach of the peace."

His impact in that tour was also shown by the way the *Sydney Sun* reported his driving ban in 1963, saying "Duggie... made more enemies down under as king of England's Rugby League 'bad men' in 1954 than any other sportsman since Harold Larwood on the bodyline cricket tour of 1932.

"His running battles in the centre made test-hardened British Lions such as Mick Sullivan, Derek Turner and company look like Little Lord Fauntleroys. Duggie's uncompromising approach was very much in evidence in the infamous abandoned New South Wales versus England clash nine years ago."

Reflecting on his 14 seasons with Saints, Duggie is on record as saying "I collected a few clouts in my time, but by God I dished a few out as well." Bearing in mind his uncompromising approach to the greatest game a fitting inscription to a possible permanent monument might be "give 'em *Mammy*, Duggie."

Appendix: Statistics and records

Club records

St Helens:
(Records courtesy Saints Heritage Society & Alex Service)

Signed for St Helens 4 February 1946 from Rivington Road School.
First team debut: 10 April 1946 away to Salford.
Final appearance: 5 December 1959 at home to Workington Town.

Appearances and tries:
Competitive matches: 484 with 186 tries, 14 goals.
(8th in all-time list of club try-scorers).
Tour matches: 5 with 1 try; Friendlies: 21.
Elected to the St Helens Hall of Fame in 1991.

Club honours:
1952-53: Lancashire Cup Final runner-up versus Leigh.
1952-53: Challenge Cup Final runner-up versus Huddersfield (captain).
1953-54: Championship Final winner versus Halifax (captain).
1953-54: Lancashire Cup Final winner versus Wigan (captain).
1955-56: Challenge Cup Final winner versus Halifax.
1956-57: Lancashire Cup Final runner-up versus Oldham.
1958-59: Lancashire Cup Final runner-up versus Oldham.
1958-59: Championship Final winner versus Hunslet.
1959-60: Lancashire Cup Final runner-up versus Warrington.

Appearances in league, cup and play-off matches:

	App	Tries	Goals
1945-46	6	1	0
1946-47	39	14	0
1947-48	35	12	0
1948-49	38	14	0
1949-50	35	11	0
1950-51	36*	9	0
1951-52	29	8	2
1952-53	41	30	11
1953-54	42	20	1
1954-55	34	7	0
1955-56	34	12	0
1956-57	24	10	0
1957-58	37	11	0
1958-59	39	22	0
1959-60	15	5	0
Totals:	**484**	**186**	**14**

* Also played in 1 abandoned match

St Helens matches versus touring teams:
1947-48 versus New Zealand
1948-49 versus Australia (1 try)
1952-53 versus Australia (captain.)
1955-56 versus New Zealand
1956-57 versus Australia

Other clubs

Wigan:
1959-60: 3 appearances, no tries or goals.

Bradford Northern:
1960-61: 4 appearances, no tries or goals.

Representative matches

Great Britain:
1951-52: 3 tests versus New Zealand, won 21-15, 20-19 and 16-12; 1 international versus France, lost 22-12.
1952-53: 2 tests versus Australia, won 21-5, lost 27-7; 1 international versus France, lost 28-17, 1 try.
1954 Tourist to Australia and New Zealand: 21 appearances, 13 tries. 1 test vs New Zealand.

England:
1951-52: versus France, lost 42-13 (Marseilles); Other Nationalities, won 31-18, 1 try (Wigan).
1952-53: versus Wales, won 19-8, 1 try (Wigan); versus France, won 15-13, 2 tries (Paris).
1953-54: versus Wales, won 24-5, 1 try (St Helens); versus Other Nationalities, won 30-22 (Wigan).

Lancashire:
1952-53: versus Cumberland, won 41-14, 1 try (St Helens); versus Australia, lost 36-11 (Warrington).
1953-54: versus Cumberland, lost 15-5 (Whitehaven).

Tour trial:
1953-54: Whites versus Reds, drew 17-17, 1 try (Leeds)

Northern Rugby League XIII:
1955-56: versus New Zealand, won 24-11, 1 try (Bradford)

Other St Helens books from London League Publications Ltd

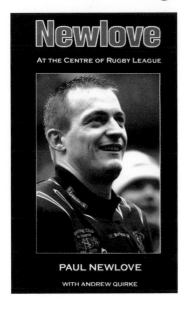

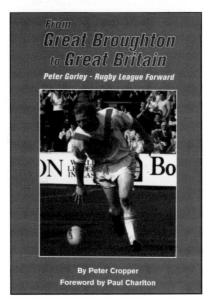

Two books about St Helens and Great Britain stars.

Now available at £5.00 each or £10.00 for the two – post free.

Order from London League Publications Ltd, PO Box 10441, London E14 8WR. Cheques payable to London League Publications Ltd, credit card orders via our website: www.llpshop.co.uk